The Quantitative Finance Interview Bible

Jean Peyre, The Quantitative Finance Interview Bible.

Paperback Edition September 2020
For any question, remark or typo please email admin@editionsducourt.com

The Quantitative Finance Interview Bible

Jean Peyre

Éditions Ducourt

Contents

Brainteasers 3
Brainteasers - Solutions 9
Stochastic Calculus 23
Stochastic Calculus - Solutions 29
Finance 41
Finance - Solutions 45
Programming 55
Programming - Solutions 59
Classic Calculations 67
Classic Calculations - Solutions 71
Math Cheatsheet 85
A Humble Request 93
   Index 95

Chapter 1

Brainteasers

Brainteasers

Difficulty: ♠ Medium ♠♠ Hard ♠♠♠ Very Hard

1.1 Triangle Impossible I ♠ (Goldman Sachs)

We randomly break a stick of length 1 into three pieces, What is the probability that the pieces can form a triangle? (breaking points are uniformly distributed between 0 and 1).

Solution in page 9

1.2 Triangle Impossible II ♠♠ (Goldman Sachs)

Let A, B and C three independent random variables uniformly distributed between 0 and 1. We make 3 sticks respectively of length A, B and C. What is the probability that the sticks can form a triangle?

Solution in page 10

1.3 A Prime Number ♠ (Commerzbank)

We consider a prime number $p \geq 5$. Prove that 24 divides $(p^2 - 1)$ i.e. $24|(p^2 - 1)$.

Solution in page 12

1.4 The Last Prime ♠ (Goldman Sachs)

Prove that there is an infinity of prime numbers.

Solution in page 12

1.5 Erdős Subsequences ♠♠♠ (Goldman Sachs)

We consider a sequence u_n, $n \in [1, 300]$ composed of distinct real numbers. Show that we can extract a strictly increasing or strictly decreasing subsequence $u_{\phi(n)}$ containing at least 17 elements.

Solution in page 12

1.6   Omelette ♠♠ (Google)

You are given two eggs, and access to a 100-storey building. Both eggs are identical. The aim is to find out the highest floor from which an egg will not break when dropped out of a window from that floor. If an egg is dropped and does not break, it is undamaged and can be dropped again. However, once an egg is broken, that's it for that egg. If an egg breaks when dropped from floor n, then it would also have broken from any floor above that. If an egg survives a fall, then it will survive any fall shorter than that.

What strategy should you adopt to minimize the number of egg drops it takes to find the solution?

Solution in page 13

1.7   A Hard Pill to Swallow ♠ (HSBC)

A blind man is alone on a deserted island. He has two blue pills and two red pills. He must take exactly one red pill and one blue pill to survive. How does he do it?

Solution in page 14

1.8   Game Theory ♠♠♠ (Goldman Sachs)

Player A invites player B to play the following game: A picks an integer n between 1 and 100, and writes it on a paper. B tries to guess n. If he succeeds, he receives n dollars. What is the fair price of the game, and what should be the strategy of B?

Solution in page 14

1.9   Stable Equilibrium I ♠ (Goldman Sachs)

N tigers circle around an antelope. If a tiger eats an antelope or another tiger, it falls asleep and it becomes a potential meal for the remaining tigers. Tigers will eat if it does not endanger their life. The antelope keeps grazing quietly. Why?

Solution in page 15

1.10   Stable Equilibrium II ♠♠ (Goldman Sachs)

100 silent monks live in a monastery with no mirrors or reflective surfaces and one important rule: no red eyes! If a monk discovers he has red eyes he commits suicide at midnight. They live happily together in peace until a tourist visiting the monastery says "at least one of you has red eyes!". What happens next?

Solution in page 15

1.11   Need For Speed ♠ (Goldman Sachs)

A car travels 100km in 1 hour. Show that, at some point, its speed was exactly 100km/h.

Solution in page 16

1.12 Russian Coin I ♠ (CitiBank)

Three players A, B and C sit around a table. They have a fair coin which gives heads or tails with a probability $\frac{1}{2}$. Player A tosses the coin, if he gets heads he wins, and the game is over. Otherwise he gives the coin to B, who is sitting at his right hand side. If B gets heads he wins, otherwise he gives the coin to C etc... What is the probability for each player to win the game?

Solution in page 16

1.13 Russian Coin II ♠ (CitiBank)

Three players A, B and C sit around a table. They have a strange coin which gives heads or tails with a probability $\frac{1}{4}$, and stays stuck on its side with a probability $\frac{1}{2}$. Player A tosses the coin, if he gets side he wins, and the game is over. Otherwise if A gets heads he gives the coin to B, who is sitting at his right hand side. If A gets tails he gives the coin to C, who is sitting at his left hand side. The next player restarts the same process. What is the probability for each player to win the game?

Solution in page 17

1.14 Be My Guest ♠♠ (Goldman Sachs)

N guests are queuing at the entrance to get seated at a wedding table. Every guest has an assigned seat number but the first guest to choose his seat is too drunk and takes a random seat. The remaining guests choose their seat according to the following rule:

- if their assigned seat is available they take it

- if their assigned seat is taken they choose randomly an available seat

What is the probability that the last person gets his assigned seat?

Solution in page 18

1.15 4 Coins, 1 Table ♠♠♠ (CitiBank)

4 coins are placed at the corners of a rotating table and the player is blindfolded. At every turn, the player can flip as many coins as he wants, and ask the game master if the coins are all showing heads. If they are all heads, the players wins, otherwise the game master can arbitrarily rotate the table before the next turn. Is there a winning strategy for the player?

Solution in page 18

1.16   N Coins, 1 Table ♠♠♠ (UBS)

2 players take turns placing coins on a large perfectly round table. Coins can not overlap and all the coin surface must be in contact with the table. The first player who can't place a coin loses. Is it better to play first and is there a winning strategy?

Solution in page 19

Chapter 2

Brainteasers - Solutions

Brainteasers - Solutions

2.1 Triangle Impossible I - Solution

Question : We randomly break a stick of length 1 into three pieces, What is the probability that the pieces can form a triangle? (breaking points are uniformly distributed between 0 and 1).

Solution : An elegant and effective method to solve the problem is to visualize it geometrically. Let us define x and y the two breaking points and let us assume $x \geq y$ (the case $x \leq y$ is symmetric). In order to form a triangle we need the longest piece to be shorter than the sum of the two other pieces.

$$\text{In the case } x \geq y \text{ we need } \begin{cases} x \geq \frac{1}{2} \\ y \leq \frac{1}{2} \\ (x - y) \leq \frac{1}{2} \end{cases} \tag{1}$$

We translate these conditions in the chart below, the chart on the left side is for the case $x \geq y$ and the chart on the right side is for the general case. The grey area represents the cases where we can form a triangle, we see that in both charts the grey area is a quarter of the full area. The probability to form a triangle is therefore $\frac{1}{4}$.

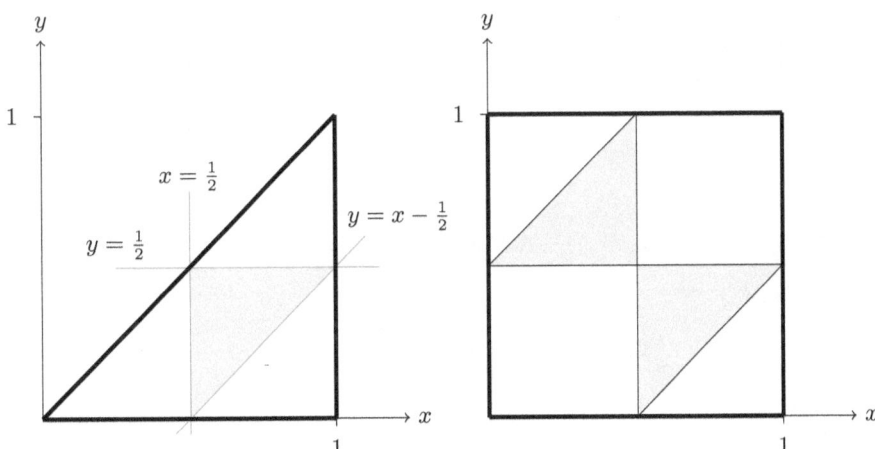

We can also answer using integrals. We consider here that $x \leq \frac{1}{2}$ (the other case is symmetric), and for $x \in [0, \frac{1}{2}]$ we see that y must be greater than $\frac{1}{2}$ and lower than $(x + \frac{1}{2})$.

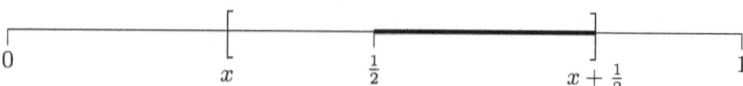

Translated into integrals, and using the symmetry argument we have P the probability to form a triangle

$$P = 2 \int\limits_{0}^{\frac{1}{2}} x\,dx = 2 \left[\frac{x^2}{2} \right]_0^{\frac{1}{2}} = \frac{1}{4}$$

2.2 Triangle Impossible II - Solution

Question : Let A, B and C three independent random variables uniformly distributed between 0 and 1. We make 3 sticks respectively of length A, B and C. What is the probability that the sticks can form a triangle?

Solution : This problem can be solved elegantly with a drawing. We work this time on a cube and the condition to form a triangle is that no stick is longer that the sum of the others.

$$\text{we need } \begin{cases} A \leq (B+C) \\ B \leq (A+C) \\ C \leq (B+A) \end{cases} \tag{2}$$

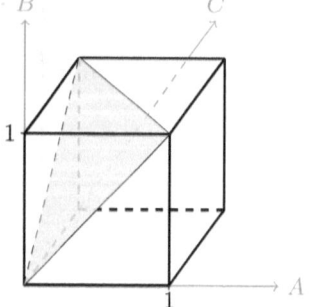
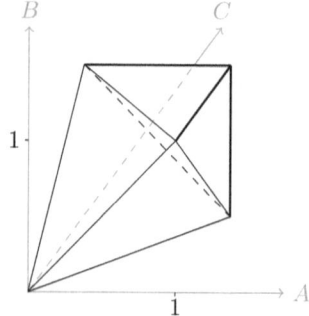

The valid volume is the diamond on the right. To calculate this volume we subtract 3 times the volume of the pyramid below from the the original cube.

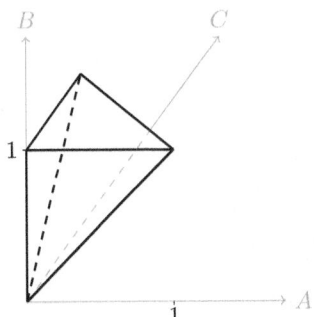

The volume of this pyramid is $V_{pyramid} = \text{base.height.}\frac{1}{3} = \frac{1}{2}.1.\frac{1}{3} = \frac{1}{6}$. Therefore $V_{diamond} = 1 - 3.\frac{3}{6} = \frac{1}{2}$. The probability we are looking for is $P = \frac{1}{2}$.

The question can also be solved with integrals

$$I = \int_{x=0}^{x=1} \int_{y=x}^{y=1} \int_{z=y}^{1\wedge(x+y)} dxdydz$$

$$I = \int_{x=0}^{x=1} \int_{y=x}^{y=1} \Big[x \wedge (1-y) \Big] dxdy$$

$$I = \int_{x=0}^{x=1} \int_{Y=0}^{Y=1-x} \Big[x \wedge Y \Big] dxdY; \quad Y = (1-y)$$

We decompose I into 3 terms

$$I = I_1 + I_2 + I_3$$

$$I = \int_{x=0}^{x=\frac{1}{2}} \int_{Y=0}^{Y=x} Y dxdY + \int_{x=0}^{x=\frac{1}{2}} \int_{Y=x}^{Y=1-x} x dxdY + \int_{x=\frac{1}{2}}^{x=1} \int_{Y=0}^{Y=1-x} Y dxdY$$

$$I_1 = \int_{x=0}^{x=\frac{1}{2}} \int_{Y=0}^{Y=x} Y dxdY = \int_{x=0}^{x=\frac{1}{2}} \frac{x^2}{2} dx$$

$$I_2 = \int_{x=0}^{x=\frac{1}{2}} \int_{Y=x}^{Y=1-x} x dxdY = \int_{x=0}^{x=\frac{1}{2}} x(1-2x) dx$$

$$I_3 = \int_{x=\frac{1}{2}}^{x=1} \int_{Y=0}^{Y=1-x} Y dxdY = \int_{x=\frac{1}{2}}^{x=1} \frac{(1-x)^2}{2} dx = \int_{s=\frac{1}{2}}^{s=0} -\frac{s^2}{2} ds = \int_{x=0}^{x=\frac{1}{2}} \frac{s^2}{2} dx$$

$$I = \int_{x=0}^{x=\frac{1}{2}} \frac{x^2}{2} + \frac{x^2}{2} + x(1-2x) dx = \int_{x=0}^{x=\frac{1}{2}} x(1-x) dx = \left[\frac{x^2}{2} - \frac{x^3}{3} \right]_0^{\frac{1}{2}} = \frac{1}{12}$$

$$P = 6I = \frac{1}{2}$$

2.3 A Prime Number - Solution

Question : We consider a prime number $p \geq 5$. Prove that 24 divides $(p^2 - 1)$ i.e. $24|(p^2 - 1)$.

Solution : In order to prove that $24|(p^2 - 1)$ we can prove that $8|(p^2 - 1)$ and $3|(p^2 - 1)$.

We note first that $p^2 - 1 = (p - 1)(p + 1)$, and p being a prime number, $(p - 1)$ and $(p + 1)$ are two consecutive even integers. Therefore both can be divided by 2 and one of them can be divided by 4. We have proved that $8|(p^2 - 1)$.

We also observe that $p - 1$, p and $p + 1$ are 3 consecutive integers. One of them is necessarily divisible by 3 and it can not be p because it is a prime number. This shows that $3|(p^2 - 1)$ and therefore $24|(p^2 - 1)$.

2.4 The Last Prime - Solution

Question : Prove that there is an infinity of prime numbers.

Solution : This is a classic proof in number theory. We proceed by contradiction, we assume that the set of all prime numbers is finite $\{n_0, n_1, ..., n_M\}$. We consider now the integer

$$K = 1 + \prod_{i=0}^{M} n_i$$

K can not be divided by any of the prime numbers in our set because for all of them we have K modulo n_i equal to 1 i.e. $K[n_i] = 1$. This means that K is a prime number which was not in our set, hence the contradiction.

2.5 Erdős Subsequences - Solution

Question : We consider a sequence u_n, $n \in [1, 300]$ composed of distinct real numbers. Show that we can extract a strictly increasing or strictly decreasing subsequence $u_{\phi(n)}$ containing at least 17 elements.

Solution : The question is about the longest monotonous subsequence that can be extracted from a given sequence. Intuitively this length increases with the length of the original sequence. We denote I_i (resp. D_i) the longest increasing (resp. decreasing) subsequence which last element is u_i. The application $i \mapsto \{I_i, D_i\}$ is injective

$$m < n \Rightarrow \begin{cases} u_m < u_n; I_n > I_m \\ \text{or} \\ u_m > u_n; D_n > D_m \end{cases}$$

Therefore once $n > p^2$ at best we can fill the square $[1, p] \times [1, p]$ and be guaranteed to find a monotonous subsequence of length $p + 1$. Actually for any n we can find a monotonous subsequence of length $\lceil \sqrt{n} \rceil$. In our case $n = 300$ and we can extract 17 ordered elements.

So why is Erdos in the title? Because the Erdős–Szekeres theorem guarantees that any sequence of distinct real numbers with length at least $(r-1)(s-1)+1$ contains a monotonically increasing subsequence of length r or a monotonically decreasing subsequence of length s. In this case $r = s = 17$ and 290 is required number in the sequence.

2.6 Omelette - Solution

Question : You are given two eggs, and access to a 100-storey building. Both eggs are identical. The aim is to find out the highest floor from which an egg will not break when dropped out of a window from that floor. If an egg is dropped and does not break, it is undamaged and can be dropped again. However, once an egg is broken, that's it for that egg. If an egg breaks when dropped from floor n, then it would also have broken from any floor above that. If an egg survives a fall, then it will survive any fall shorter than that.

What strategy should you adopt to minimize the number of egg drops it takes to find the solution?

Solution : The objective is to minimize the number of attempts in the worst case. If we had only one egg to solve the problem we would have needed to start at the first floor and to go up one floor for every new attempt. In the worst case we would have needed 100 attempts. If we have 2 eggs we can improve this strategy and skip floors when using the first egg. If the first egg breaks we can single out an interval of floors. We can then use the second egg to test the floors in the interval one by one from the bottom. The crucial question is the choice of intervals to skip with the first egg. We denote u_i the sequence of floors from which the first egg is thrown and $W(k)$ the number of attempts needed in the worst case to solve the problem with 2 eggs and k floors. After the first attempt at u_1, if the egg breaks we need try all the floors between 1 and $u_i - 1$. Otherwise we still have 2 eggs and $(100 - u_i)$ remaining floors to test

$$W(100) = \max\left(u_1, 1 + W(100 - u_1)\right)$$

we repeat the same reasoning until the ith floor

$$W(100) = \max\left(u_1, u_2 - u_1 + 1, u_3 - u_2 + 2, \ldots, 1 + W(100 - u_i)\right)$$

we denote v_i the increments sequence $v_i = u_i - u_{i-1}$, and $v_1 = u_1$. The equation becomes

$$W(100) = \max\left(v_1, v2 + 1, v_3 + 3, \ldots, 1 + W\left(100 - \sum_{k=1}^{i} v_k\right)\right)$$

and the full formula for the number of attempts is

$$W(100) = \max\left(v_1, v2 + 1, v_3 + 2, \ldots, v_n + n - 1\right)$$

we minimize this maximum when all the arguments are equal. On the other hand the increments sum to 100

$$\sum_{k=1}^{n} v_k = 100$$

We denote $M = v_i + i - 1$, and for a given n the condition on M is

$$\sum_{k=1}^{n}(M - k + 1) = nM + n - \sum_{k=1}^{n}k > 100$$

$$M > \frac{100}{n} - 1 + \frac{n+1}{2}$$

we calculate the derivative of the right side to find that the minimum is reached for $n = \sqrt{200} \approx 14.14$ and therefore $M = 15$. In the worst case we will need 15 attempts and the sequence of floors to test with the first egg is

$$15, 29, 42, 54, 65, 75, 84, 92, 99, 100$$

2.7 A Hard Pill to Swallow - Solution

Question : A blind man is alone on a deserted island. He has two blue pills and two red pills. He must take exactly one red pill and one blue pill to survive. How does he do it?

Solution : Break each of the pills in half, as you do this pop one half in your mouth and discard the other half.

2.8 Game Theory - Solution

Question : Player A invites player B to play the following game: A picks an integer n between 1 and 100, and writes it on a paper. B tries to guess n. If he succeeds, he receives n dollars. What is the fair price of the game, and what should be the strategy of B?

Solution : A tempting strategy for player A is to pick the lowest number 1 and to be guaranteed to lose at most 1. The expected loss of the winning strategy will have to be lower than 1. The key in this type of question is to observe that both players have access to the same amount of information. Therefore player B will guess the optimal strategy of A and take full advantage of it. We denote $p(i)$ the discrete probability distribution that A decides to use i for his choice. When player B picks a number he has an expected gain equal to $g_i = p(i).i$. Remember that player B will guess the probability distribution p, he will try to maximize his gain and player A will minimize the quantity

$$M = \max_{i \in [1,100]} g_i$$

This maximum is minimized when all the elements are equal $p(i).i = \lambda$. We find λ using the probability distribution properties

$$\sum_{1}^{100} p(i) = \sum_{1}^{100} \frac{\lambda}{i} = 1$$

$$\lambda = \frac{1}{\sum_{1}^{100} \frac{1}{i}} \approx \frac{1}{1 + \ln(n)}$$

therefore player A will pick the number i with a probability $p(i) = \frac{\lambda}{i}$. The expected loss (gain) for A (B) is $G = p(i).i = \lambda$. The numerical application with 100 numbers gives $G \approx 0.18$.

2.9 Stable Equilibrium I - Solution

Question : N tigers circle around an antelope. If a tiger eats an antelope or another tiger, it falls asleep and it becomes a potential meal for the remaining tigers. Tigers will eat if it does not endanger their life. The antelope keeps grazing quietly. Why?

Solution : In this classic type of question an unexpected equilibrium appears in a system. The best way to understand it is to start with a small number of tigers.

- 1 tiger: the tiger clearly eats the antelope, he does not need to worry about sleeping after the meal.

- 2 tigers: if a tiger eats the antelope he gets eaten by the other tiger. Tigers know that and decide to stay still. The system with 2 tigers is a stable system.

- 3 tigers: tigers have read this book and know that the 2 tigers system is stable, one of them eats the antelope, falls asleep and becomes the pray in a stable 2 tigers system.

- 4 tigers: tigers know that the 3 tigers system is unstable and prefer not to eat the antelope, the 4 tigers system is stable.

It appears that systems with an even number of tigers are stable. The antelope is relaxed because she has counted the tigers and found an even number.

2.10 Stable Equilibrium II - Solution

Question : 100 silent monks live in a monastery with no mirrors or reflective surfaces and one important rule: no red eyes! If a monk discovers he has red eyes he commits suicide at midnight. They live happily together in peace until a tourist visiting the monastery says "at least one of you has red eyes!". What happens next?

Solution : This is a different version of a classic type of equilibrium puzzles. We start with the cases with a low number of red eyed monks (RE group).

- Zero RE monk and the tourist lied to them: on the first day all the monks think that they are RE because they cannot see anyone else in RE. At midnight they all commit suicide. This bad prank should not happen because the tourist is assumed to tell the truth.

- 1 RE monk: the RE monk cannot see anyone else in RE and commits suicide at midnight.

- 2 RE monks: RE monks think on the first day that there is only one RE monk and they can see it. But no one commits suicide on the first night. At that point they realize that they are in a system with 2 RE and they both commit suicide on the second night.

- 3 RE monks: RE monks think that they are in a system with 2 RE, but no one commits suicide on the second night, they realize that it is a 3 RE system and they all commit suicide on the third night.

The pattern is clear, in conclusion in a system with j RE monks, all the RE monks commit suicide on the jth night.

2.11 Need For Speed - Solution

Question : A car travels 100km in 1 hour. Show that, at some point, its speed was exactly 100km/h.

Solution : This is a recurrent type of question based on the continuity of a function or its derivative. We denote $x(t)$ the position of the car at time t. $x(0) = 0$, $x(1) = 100$ and the mean value theorem proves that

$$\exists c \in [0,1]: \quad x'(c) = \frac{x(1) - x(0)}{1} = 100$$

Alternatively we can use the intermediate value theorem, if the average speed is 100, the speed cannot always be higher than 100, and it cannot always be lower than 100. There exists therefore a moment t_h where the speed is greater or equal to 100 and a moment t_l where the speed is lower or equal 100. Therefore $x'(t_h) \geq 100$ and $x'(t_l) \leq 100$ and $\exists c : x'(c) = 100$.

2.12 Russian Coin I - Solution

Question : Three players A, B and C sit around a table. They have a fair coin which gives heads or tails with a probability $\frac{1}{2}$. Player A tosses the coin, if he gets heads he wins, and the game is over. Otherwise he gives the coin to B, who is sitting at his right hand side. If B gets heads he wins, otherwise he gives the coin to C etc... What is the probability for each player to win the game?

Solution : There is an elegant way to solve this problem based on the symmetry of the players position. We define p_A (resp. p_B, p_C) the probability that player A (resp. B, C) wins the game and p as follows

$$p = P\{\text{Player who starts wins the game}\}$$

we see clearly that $p_A = p$. By symmetry, f player A misses his first toss player B finds himself in the position of starting the same game. Therefore

$$p_B = P\{\text{A misses the first toss} \cap \text{Player who starts wins the game}\} = \frac{p}{2}$$

$$p_C = \frac{p}{4}$$

Also the probability that no one wins is zero

$$P\{\text{No one wins}\} = \lim_{\infty} \frac{1}{2}^n = 0$$

and

$$p_A + p_B + p_C = p + \frac{p}{2} + \frac{p}{4} = 1$$

$$p = \frac{4}{7} = p_A; \quad p_B = \frac{2}{7}; \quad p_C = \frac{1}{7}$$

The question can also be solved with series. We find that

$$p_A = \frac{1}{2} + \frac{1}{2} \cdot \frac{1}{2}^3 + \cdots + \frac{1}{2} \cdot \frac{1}{2}^{3i}$$

$$p_A = \frac{1}{2} \sum_{i=0}^{\infty} \frac{1}{8}^i = \frac{1}{2} \frac{1}{1 - \frac{1}{8}} = \frac{4}{7}$$

2.13 Russian Coin II - Solution

Question : Three players A, B and C sit around a table. They have a strange coin which gives heads or tails with a probability $\frac{1}{4}$, and stays stuck on its side with a probability $\frac{1}{2}$. Player A tosses the coin, if he gets side he wins, and the game is over. Otherwise if A gets heads he gives the coin to B, who is sitting at his right hand side. If A gets tails he gives the coin to C, who is sitting at his left hand side. The next player restarts the same process. What is the probability for each player to win the game?

Solution : We denote $P(i|j)$ the probability of the player j winning a game started by the player i. The probability of no one winning is equal to zero

$$P\{\text{No one wins}\} = \lim_{\infty} \frac{1}{2}^n = 0$$

therefore

$$P(A|A) + P(B|A) + P(C|A) = 1$$

We can visualize the possible outcomes after A turn

A plays $\begin{cases} \text{A gets heads with a probability } \frac{1}{4}; \text{ B wins with a probability } P(B|B) \\ \text{A gets tails with a probability } \frac{1}{4}; \text{ B wins with a probability } P(B|C) \\ \text{A gets side with a probability } \frac{1}{2}; \text{ A wins} \end{cases}$

and

$$P(B|A) = \frac{1}{4}P(B|B) + \frac{1}{4}P(B|C)$$

and by symmetry $P(B|B) = P(A|A)$ and $P(B|C) = P(C|A)$ giving

$$P(B|A) = \frac{1}{4}P(A|A) + \frac{1}{4}P(C|A)$$

By symmetry we also have

$$P(B|A) = P(C|A)$$

so the system of equations is

$$P(A|A) + 2P(B|A) = 1$$

$$\frac{3}{4}P(B|A) = \frac{1}{4}P(A|A)$$

We find $P(A|A) = \frac{3}{5}$ and $P(B|A) = P(C|A) = \frac{1}{5}$.

2.14 Be My Guest - Solution

Question : N guests are queuing at the entrance to get seated at a wedding table. Every guest has an assigned seat number but the first guest to choose his seat is too drunk and takes a random seat. The remaining guests choose their seat according to the following rule:

- if their assigned seat is available they take it

- if their assigned seat is taken they choose randomly an available seat

What is the probability that the last person gets his assigned seat?

Solution : Let us say the drunk person's seat is the number 1 and the last person's assigned seat is n. If at any moment a displaced person randomly chooses the seat number n, then the last person cannot get his assigned seat. But the critical remark is that, if at any time a displaced person randomly chooses the seat number 1, then the last person get his assigned seat. The chain of displaced guests is a cyclical permutation of the chain of assigned seats and choosing the seat 1 closes the cycle.

Guest	k	1	i	j
Seat	1	i	j	k

Therefore, as long as the seats 1 and n are available, the entering guest k has the following options

$$\begin{cases} p = \frac{1}{k} \text{ to pick 1, the last person is not displaced} \\ p = \frac{1}{k} \text{ to pick n, the last person is displaced} \\ p = \frac{k-2}{k} \text{ to pick another seat, the choice between 1 and n is postponed} \end{cases}$$

we can ignore how often the choice between 1 and n is postponed, when it finally happens the probabilities to choose 1 or n are equal. The probability that the last person gets his assigned seat is $\frac{1}{2}$.

2.15 4 Coins, 1 Table - Solution

Question : 4 coins are placed at the corners of a rotating table and the player is blindfolded. At every turn, the player can flip as many coins as he wants, and ask the game master if the coins are all showing heads. If they are all heads, the players wins, otherwise the game master can arbitrarily rotate the table before the next turn. Is there a winning strategy for the player?

Solution : We use the notation [h,h,h,t] for the current coins position, where h stands for heads and t for tails. We group the coins positions in classes which are stable by cyclical permutation. That means for example that [t,h,h,h], [h,t,h,h], [h,h,t,h] are grouped in the same class. Each time the player asks the game master if the current position is a winning position he can also flip all the coins and test the complementary position too. Therefore we can include the complementary sets in the classes, which means that [t,h,h,h], [h,t,t,t], [h,t,h,h], [t,h,t,t] etc... are in a same class.

We use the notation [f,o,o,o] to indicate which coins are flipped by the player, f stands for flipped and o indicates that the coins are not flipped. Similarly we group the player moves in classes which are stable by cyclical permutation.

$$
\text{Position Classes} \begin{cases} p_1 : [h,h,h,h] \\ p_2 : [t,h,h,h] \\ p_3 : [t,t,h,h] \\ p_4 : [t,h,t,h] \end{cases} \quad \text{Transition Classes} \begin{cases} t_1 : [f,f,f,f] \\ t_2 : [f,o,o,o] \\ t_3 : [f,f,o,o] \\ t_4 : [f,o,f,o] \end{cases}
$$

The transition t_1 is used at every step to check the complementary position. The position class p_1 is a winning position. We draw the following transition diagram

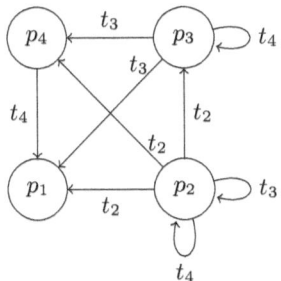

We notice that the transition t_4 applied on p_4 always leads to p_1. We can also see that p_2 and p_3 are stable by t_4. Note that the diagram does not include some adverse transitions, for example t_2 applied to p_4 sends back to p_2. But we can find a winning strategy with the information available in the diagram

- We ask if the starting position is a winning one. If not we are not in p_1

- We start by applying t_4. If we land in a winning position then we were in p_4. If not, we are either in p_2 or p_3.

- We apply now t_3 and then t_4. If we land in a winning position (after applying t_3 or after applying t_4) we can confirm we were in p_3 otherwise it means we were in p_2

- We know now that we are in p_2. We apply t_2, t_3 and t_4 to win.

The winning algorithm including the complementary check is therefore

$$
t_4, t_1, t_3, t_1, t_4, t_1, t_2, t_1, t_3, t_1, t_4, t_1
$$

2.16   N Coins, 1 Table - Solution

Question :   2 players take turns placing coins on a large perfectly round table. Coins can not overlap and all the coin surface must be in contact with the table. The first player who can't place a coin loses. Is it better to play first and is there a winning strategy?

Solution : The table is round and the winning strategy in this game is based on the central symmetry of the table. The first player A places his coin at the exact center of the table. Every time B places a coin A can respond by placing his coin in the symmetric position. With this strategy B is forced to discover new areas and A is guaranteed to place a coin. Therefore B will eventually run out of space and A is certain to win.

Chapter 3

Stochastic Calculus

Stochastic Calculus

3.1 Lognormal Expectation ♠ (Natixis)

Calculate $\mathbb{E}\left(\exp(X)\right)$ when is X is a normally distributed random variable

$$X \sim \mathcal{N}\left(\mu, \sigma^2\right)$$

Solution in page 29

3.2 Cumulative Brownian ♠ (Deutsche Bank)

Calculate $\mathbb{E}(\Phi(B_t))$ where B_t a brownian motion and Φ the standard normal cumulative distribution.

Solution in page 30

3.3 Multiplicative Itô ♠ (BNP)

For each of the processes X_t below find the process $a(s, \omega)$ such that

$$X_t = E[X_t] + \int_0^t a \, dB_s$$

i) $X_t = B_t^2$ iii) $X_t = e^{B_t}$

ii) $X_t = B_t^3$ iv) $X_t = \sin B_t$

Solution in page 30

3.4 Two Sided Corridor ♠♠ (BNP)

Let B_t be a Brownian Motion and u and d two positive real numbers. We consider an option which pays 1 if B_t reaches u and remained greater then $-d$ since inception

$$\exists t_0 : B_{t_0} = u; \ \forall t \in [0, t_0], B_t > -d$$

payment is made when the barrier is touched. Calculate the price of this option when rates are zero. Calculate the average exit time i.e. the average time before touching u or $-d$.

Solution in page 32

3.5   One sided corridor ♠♠ (BNP)

Let B_t be a Brownian Motion and u a positive real number. We consider an option which pays 1 if B_t reaches u

$$\exists t_0 : B_{t_0} = u; \ \forall t \in [0, t_0], B_t > -d$$

payment is made when the barrier is touched. Calculate the price of this option when rates are zero and with rates $r > 0$.

Solution in page 33

3.6   Two Sided Corridor With Rates ♠♠ (BNP)

Let B_t be a Brownian Motion and u and d two positive real numbers. We consider an option which pays 1 if B_t reaches u and remained greater then $-d$ since inception

$$\exists t_0 : B_{t_0} = u; \ \forall t \in [0, t_0], B_t > -d$$

payment is made when the barrier is touched. Calculate the price of this option with rates $r > 0$.

Solution in page 33

3.7   Bouncing Corridor ♠♠♠ (BNP)

Let B_t be a Brownian Motion and u and d two positive real numbers. We consider an option which pays 1 if B_t reaches u and touched the down barrier before. The option is knocked out and pays zero if it touches the up barrier first.

$$\text{pays 1 if } \exists t_0 : B_{t_0} = u; \ \exists t_1 \in [0, t_0] : B_{t_1} = -d$$

$$\text{pays 0 if } \exists t_0 : B_{t_0} = u; \ \forall t \in [0, t_0], B_t > -d$$

payment is made when the barrier is touched. Calculate the price of this option with rates $r > 0$. Generalize to an option paying 1 after n bounces (pays 1 if the option touches u then u then $-d$ etc... n times, pays 0 if u is touched first).

Solution in page 34

3.8   Brownian Bridge ♠ (JP Morgan)

Let B_s be a Brownian bridge, that is a Brownian motion constrained such that $B_0 = 0$ and $B_t = x$. What is the distribution of B_s, for $0 \le s < t$?

Solution in page 35

3.9   Martingales? ♠ (Societe Generale)

Are the following processes martingales?

i) $X_t = B_t + 8t$

iii) $X_t = B_t^3$

ii) $X_t = B_t^2$

iv) $X_t = t^2 B_t - 2 \int_0^t s B_s ds$

Solution in page 36

3.10 Natural Martingale ♠♠♠ (JP Morgan)

Let Y be a real valued random variable on $(\Omega, \mathcal{F}, P)$ such that

$$E[|Y|] < \infty$$

Define

$$M_t = E[Y|\mathcal{F}_t]; \quad t \geq 0$$

Show that M_t is an $\mathcal{F}_t$-martingale. Conversely, let $M_t; t \geq 0$ be a real valued $\mathcal{F}_t$-martingale such that

$$\sup_{t \geq 0} E\left[|M_t|^p\right] < \infty \quad \text{for some} \quad p > 1$$

Show that there exists $Y \in L^1(P)$ such that $M_t = E[Y|\mathcal{F}_t]$.

Solution in page 37

3.11 Exponential Brownian ♠♠ (JP Morgan)

Let B_t be Brownian motion on $\mathbf{R}$, $B_0 = 0$. Prove that

$$\mathbb{E}\left[e^{iuB_t}\right] = \exp\left(-\frac{1}{2}u^2 t\right) \quad \text{for all} \quad u \in \mathbf{R}$$

Use the power series expansion of the exponential function on both sides, compare the terms with the same power of u and deduce that

$$\mathbb{E}\left[B_t^4\right] = 3t^2$$

and more generally that

$$\mathbb{E}\left[B_t^{2k}\right] = \frac{(2k)!}{2^k \cdot k!} t^k; \quad k \in \mathbf{N}$$

Solution in page 38

Chapter 4

Stochastic Calculus - Solutions

Stochastic Calculus - Solutions

4.1 Lognormal Expectation - Solution

Question : Calculate $\mathbb{E}\left(\exp(X)\right)$ when is X is a normally distributed random variable

$$X \sim \mathcal{N}\left(\mu, \sigma^2\right)$$

Solution : The result can be found elegantly, we know that Y_t is a martingale where

$$Y_t = \exp\left(-\frac{\sigma^2}{2}t + \sigma B_t\right) = \exp\left(-\frac{\sigma^2}{2}t + \sigma\sqrt{t}Z\right)$$

where Z is a standard normal distribution. $X' = \mu + \sigma Z$ has the same distribution as X, we set $t = 1$

$$\mathbb{E}(Y_1) = \mathbb{E}(Y_0) = 1 = \exp\left(-\frac{\sigma^2}{2} - \mu\right)\mathbb{E}\left(\exp\left(\mu + \sigma Z\right)\right)$$

and therefore

$$\mathbb{E}\left(\exp(X)\right) = \exp\left(\frac{\sigma^2}{2} + \mu\right)$$

The expectation can also be calculated using integrals

$$\mathbb{E}\left(\exp(X)\right) = \int_{-\infty}^{\infty} \exp(x)\frac{1}{\sqrt{2\pi}\sigma}\exp\left(-\frac{(x-\mu)^2}{2\sigma^2}\right)dx$$

$$\mathbb{E}\left(\exp(X)\right) = \frac{1}{\sqrt{2\pi}\sigma}\int_{-\infty}^{\infty}\exp\left(\frac{2\sigma^2 x - x^2 + 2\mu x - \mu^2}{2\sigma^2}\right)dx$$

$$\mathbb{E}\left(\exp(X)\right) = \frac{1}{\sqrt{2\pi}\sigma}\int_{-\infty}^{\infty}\exp\left(\frac{-\left(x - \left(\sigma^2 + \mu\right)\right)^2}{2\sigma^2} + \frac{\sigma^4 + 2\mu\sigma^2}{2\sigma^2}\right)dx$$

$$\mathbb{E}\left(\exp(X)\right) = \exp\left(\frac{\sigma^2}{2} + \mu\right)\int_{-\infty}^{\infty}\frac{1}{\sqrt{2\pi}\sigma}\exp\left(\frac{-\left(x - \left(\sigma^2 + \mu\right)\right)^2}{2\sigma^2}\right)dx$$

We identify the integral of the density of a normal distribution, equal to 1 and

$$\mathbb{E}\left(\exp(X)\right) = \exp\left(\frac{\sigma^2}{2} + \mu\right)$$

4.2 Cumulative Brownian - Solution

Question : Calculate $\mathbb{E}(\Phi(B_t))$ where B_t a brownian motion and Φ the standard normal cumulative distribution.

Solution : The elegant solution for this problem is based on the symmetry of the brownian motion:

$$\mathbb{E}\left(\Phi\left(W_t\right)\right) = \mathbb{E}\left(\Phi\left(-W_t\right)\right) = \mathbb{E}\left(1 - \Phi\left(W_t\right)\right) = 1 - \mathbb{E}\left(\Phi\left(W_t\right)\right)$$

and we get

$$\mathbb{E}\left(\Phi\left(W_t\right)\right) = \frac{1}{2}$$

The result can also be proved using integrals

$$\mathbb{E}\left(\Phi\left(W_t\right)\right) = \int_{-\infty}^{+\infty} \left(\int_{-\infty}^{x} \frac{1}{\sqrt{2\pi}} \exp\left(\frac{-u^2}{2}\right) du\right) \frac{1}{\sqrt{2\pi t}} \exp\left(\frac{-x^2}{2t}\right) dt$$

$$\mathbb{E}\left(\Phi\left(W_t\right)\right) = \int_{-\infty}^{+\infty} \Phi(x)\Phi'(x)dx = \left[\frac{\Phi^2(x)}{2}\right]_{-\infty}^{+\infty} = \frac{1}{2}$$

4.3 Multiplicative Itô- Solution

Question : For each of the processes X_t below find the process $a(s,\omega)$ such that

$$X_t = E[X_t] + \int_0^t a dB_s$$

i) $X_t = B_t^2$

iii) $X_t = e^{B_t}$

ii) $X_t = B_t^3$

iv) $X_t = \sin B_t$

Solution :

i) $X_t = B_t^2$

We apply Itô's formula to find the dynamics of X_t

$$dX_t = 2B_t dB_t + dt$$

$$X_t = t + \int_0^t 2B_s dB_s$$

Which corresponds to the required decomposition with

$$E[X_t] = t; \quad a = 2B_s$$

ii) $X_t = B_t^3$

By applying Itô's formula we get

$$dX_t = 3B_t^2 dB_t + 3B_t dt$$

we need to decompose further the term $3B_t dt$, we consider the process $Y_t = tB_t$

$$dY_t = B_t dt + t dB_t$$

$$Y_t = \int_0^t B_s ds + \int_0^t s dB_s$$

therefore

$$\int_0^t B_s ds = tB_t - \int_0^t s dB_s$$

we can reinject this equation in X_t

$$X_t = \int_0^t 3B_s^2 dB_s + 3tB_t - 3\int_0^t s dB_s$$

$$X_t = \int_0^t 3B_s^2 dB_s + 3t\int_0^t dB_s - 3\int_0^t s dB_s$$

giving the desired decomposition with

$$\mathbb{E}[X_t] = 0; \quad a = 3B_s^2 + 3(t - s)$$

iii) $X_t = e^{B_t}$

We apply Itô's formula to find the dynamics of X_t

$$dX_t = e^{B_t} dB_t + \frac{1}{2}e^{B_t} dt$$

We can eliminate the term in dt with a classic technique used for Ornsetin Uhlenbeck derivation (see page 67). We denote A a constant and we consider the process $Y_t = e^{At}e^{B_t}$

$$dY_t = e^{B_t}e^{At} dB_t + \frac{1}{2}e^{B_t}e^{At} dt + Ae^{B_t}e^{At} dt$$

we choose $A = -\frac{1}{2}$ and we get

$$d\left(e^{B_t}e^{\frac{-t}{2}}\right) = e^{B_t}e^{\frac{-t}{2}} dB_t$$

$$e^{B_t}e^{\frac{-t}{2}} - 1 = \int_0^t e^{B_s}e^{\frac{-s}{2}} dB_s$$

and

$$e^{B_t} = e^{\frac{t}{2}} + \int_0^t e^{B_s + \frac{t-s}{2}} dB_s$$

giving the decomposition

$$\mathbb{E}[X_t] = e^{\frac{t}{2}}; \quad a = e^{B_s + \frac{t-s}{2}}$$

iv) $X_t = \sin B_t$

We start with Itô's formula to find the dynamics of X_t

$$dX_t = \cos B_t dB_t - \frac{1}{2} \sin B_t dt$$

We can eliminate the term in dt by introducing $Y_t = e^{\frac{t}{2}} \sin B_t$ (see previous case).

$$d\left(\sin B_t e^{\frac{t}{2}}\right) = \cos B_t e^{\frac{t}{2}} dB_t$$

and

$$\sin B_t = \int_0^t \cos B_s e^{\frac{s-t}{2}} dB_s$$

giving the decomposition

$$\mathbb{E}[X_t] = 0; \quad a = \cos B_s e^{\frac{s-t}{2}}$$

4.4 Two Sided Corridor - Solution

Question : Let B_t be a Brownian Motion and u and d two positive real numbers. We consider an option which pays 1 if B_t reaches u and remained greater then $-d$ since inception

$$\exists t_0 : B_{t_0} = u; \ \forall t \in [0, t_0], B_t > -d$$

payment is made when the barrier is touched. Calculate the price of this option when rates are zero. Calculate the average exit time i.e. the average time before touching u or $-d$.

Solution : This is a classic application of the optional sampling theorem (see page 87). We define τ the first hitting time of u or $-d$. τ is a stopping time. The process $B_{\tau \wedge t}$ is a bounded martingale. By applying the optional sampling theorem to $B_{\tau \wedge t}$ and τ we obtain

$$\mathbb{E}\left(B_{\tau \wedge \tau}\right) = \mathbb{E}\left(B_\tau\right) = \mathbb{E}\left(B_0\right) = 0$$

and

$$\mathbb{E}\left(B_\tau\right) = p.u - (1-p).d = 0$$

where p is the probability to hit u first. The price of the option is therefore

$$\text{Price} = P\left\{\text{hit } u \text{ first}\right\} = \frac{d}{u+d}$$

4.5   One Sided Corridor - Solution

Question :   Let B_t be a Brownian Motion and u a positive real number. We consider an option which pays 1 if B_t reaches u

$$\exists t_0 : B_{t_0} = u; \ \forall t \in [0, t_0], B_t > -d$$

payment is made when the barrier is touched. Calculate the price of this option when rates are zero and with rates $r > 0$.

Solution :   In this version of the question the stopped Brownian motion is not bounded and we cannot directly apply the optional sampling theorem. Actually the probability of reaching u is 1 because the probability of the brownian motion reaching any given point is 1 (see page 87). The price of the option without rates is 1. When interest rates are applied we need to evaluate $\mathbb{E}\left(\exp\left(-r\tau_u\right)\right)$ where τ_u is the first hitting time of u. In order to evaluate it we consider the martingale

$$X_t = \exp\left(aB_t - \frac{a^2}{2}t\right)$$

with $a > 0$. The process $X_{\tau \wedge t}$ is a bounded martingale. By applying the optional sampling theorem (see page optstop) to $X_{\tau_u \wedge t}$ and τ_u we obtain

$$\mathbb{E}\left(X_{\tau_u \wedge \tau_u}\right) = \mathbb{E}\left(X_{\tau_u}\right) = \mathbb{E}\left(X_0\right) = 1$$

and

$$\mathbb{E}\left(X_{\tau_u}\right) = \mathbb{E}\left(\exp\left(a.u - \frac{a^2}{2}\tau_u\right)\right) = 1$$

$$\mathbb{E}\left(\exp\left(-\frac{a^2}{2}\tau_u\right)\right) = \exp\left(-a.u\right)$$

We set $a = \sqrt{2r}$ to find the option price

$$\text{Price} = \mathbb{E}\left(\exp\left(-r\tau_u\right)\right) = \exp\left(-\sqrt{2r}.u\right)$$

NB. The one-sided version of the corridor can be a confusing question. It is sometimes asked differently with a stock following brownian motion dynamics, starting in A and paying 1 if the stock reaches $B > A$. The interviewer often assumes that the process behaves like a stock in the sense that if it touches zero the process stays at zero (the stock of a company is equal to zero in case of default). That version is equivalent to a double sided corridor between 0 and B.

4.6   Two Sided Corridor With Rates - Solution

Question :   Let B_t be a Brownian Motion and u and d two positive real numbers. We consider an option which pays 1 if B_t reaches u and remained greater then $-d$ since inception

$$\exists t_0 : B_{t_0} = u; \ \forall t \in [0, t_0], B_t > -d$$

payment is made when the barrier is touched. Calculate the price of this option with rates $r > 0$.

Solution :   We define τ the first hitting time of u or $-d$. Let U be the subset of Ω where u is hit first and D be the subset where $-d$ is hit first. We need to evaluate $\mathbb{E}\left(\mathbb{1}_U \exp\left(-r\tau\right)\right)$. We consider the martingale

$$X_t = \exp\left(-rt + \sqrt{2r}B_t\right)$$

$X_{\tau \wedge t}$ is a bounded martingale. By applying the optional sampling theorem (see page 87) to $X_{\tau_u \wedge t}$ and τ_u we obtain

$$\mathbb{E}(X_\tau) = \mathbb{E}\left(\mathbb{1}_U \exp\left(-r\tau + \sqrt{2r}u\right)\right) + \mathbb{E}\left(\mathbb{1}_D \exp\left(-r\tau - \sqrt{2r}d\right)\right) = 1$$

But this is also true for the process

$$Y_t = \exp\left(-rt - \sqrt{2r}B_t\right)$$

yielding the equation system

$$\exp\left(\sqrt{2r}u\right) A_u + \exp\left(-\sqrt{2r}d\right) A_d = 1$$

$$\exp\left(-\sqrt{2r}u\right) A_u + \exp\left(\sqrt{2r}d\right) A_d = 1$$

where $A_u = \mathbb{E}\left(\mathbb{1}_U \exp\left(-r\tau\right)\right)$ and $A_d = \mathbb{E}\left(\mathbb{1}_D \exp\left(-r\tau\right)\right)$. Solving the system we find

$$A_u = \frac{\sinh\left(\sqrt{2r}u\right)}{\sinh\left(\sqrt{2r}(u+d)\right)}$$

$$A_d = \frac{\sinh\left(\sqrt{2r}d\right)}{\sinh\left(\sqrt{2r}(u+d)\right)}$$

and in this case

$$\text{Price} = A_u = \mathbb{E}\left(\mathbb{1}_U \exp\left(-r\tau\right)\right)$$

4.7   Bouncing Corridor - Solution

Question :   Let B_t be a Brownian Motion and u and d two positive real numbers. We consider an option which pays 1 if B_t reaches u and touched the down barrier before. The option is knocked out and pays zero if it touches the up barrier first.

$$\text{pays 1 if } \exists t_0 : B_{t_0} = u; \ \exists t_1 \in [0, t_0] : B_{t_1} = -d$$

$$\text{pays 0 if } \exists t_0 : B_{t_0} = u; \ \forall t \in [0, t_0], B_t > -d$$

payment is made when the barrier is touched. Calculate the price of this option with rates $r > 0$. Generalize to an option paying 1 after n bounces (pays 1 if the option touches u then u then $-d$ etc... n times, pays 0 if u is touched first).

Solution :   We define τ the first hitting time of u or $-d$. τ is a stopping time. If u is touched first the payoff is zero. If $-d$ is touched first the option becomes similar to the one sided barrier case with an upper barrier at $(u + d)$. The price of that option was calculated in 3.5

$$\text{Price}_{\text{one sided}} = \exp\left(-\sqrt{2r}(u + d)\right)$$

and the price of the bouncing option is

$$\text{Price} = \exp\left(-\sqrt{2r}(u + d)\right) \mathbb{E}\left(\mathbb{1}_D \exp\left(-r\tau\right)\right)$$

where D be the subset where $-d$ is hit first. The expectation term was calculated in the question 3.6 and we get

$$\text{Price} = \exp\left(-\sqrt{2r}(u + d)\right) \frac{\sinh\left(\sqrt{2r}d\right)}{\sinh\left(\sqrt{2r}(u + d)\right)}$$

To generalize we add one bounce, we consider an option paying 1 if the process touches consecutively u, $-d$ and u. In this case when u is touched we have a new type of option. We will receive 1 after the down barrier and the up barrier are touched consecutively but there is no knockout feature. We price this option first. We consider a different Brownian Motion W_t starting at 0 and paying 1 if a down barrier at $(-u - d)$ is touched and W_t returns to 0. We denote $\tilde{\tau}$ the first hitting time of $(-u - d)$.

$$\text{Price}_{\text{no knockout}} = \exp\left(-\sqrt{2r}(u + d)\right) \mathbb{E}\left(\exp\left(-r\tilde{\tau}\right)\right)$$

$$\text{Price}_{\text{no knockout}} = \exp\left(-2\sqrt{2r}(u + d)\right)$$

and the price of the option with 2 bounces is

$$\text{Price}_{2 \text{ bounces}} = \exp\left(-2\sqrt{2r}(u + d)\right) \mathbb{E}\left(\mathbb{1}_U \exp\left(-r\tau\right)\right)$$

$$\text{Price}_{2 \text{ bounces}} = \exp\left(-2\sqrt{2r}(u + d)\right) \frac{\sinh\left(\sqrt{2r}u\right)}{\sinh\left(\sqrt{2r}(u + d)\right)}$$

and generalizing to n bounces, if the first triggering barrier is up

$$\text{Price}_{n \text{ bounces}} = \exp\left(-n\sqrt{2r}(u + d)\right) \frac{\sinh\left(\sqrt{2r}u\right)}{\sinh\left(\sqrt{2r}(u + d)\right)}$$

and when the first triggering barrier is down

$$\text{Price}_{n \text{ bounces}} = \exp\left(-n\sqrt{2r}(u + d)\right) \frac{\sinh\left(\sqrt{2r}d\right)}{\sinh\left(\sqrt{2r}(u + d)\right)}$$

4.8 Brownian Bridge - Solution

Question : Let B_s be a Brownian bridge, that is a Brownian motion constrained such that $B_0 = 0$ and $B_t = x$. What is the distribution of B_s, for $0 \leq s < t$?

Solution : We are looking for the distribution of B_s. We denote $\Delta y = [y, y + dy]$ and we consider the infinitesimal probability

$$\mathbb{P}\left(B_s \in \Delta y | B_t \in \Delta x \text{ and } B_0 = 0\right)$$

B_0 is deterministic, we apply Bayes Formula (see page 88)

$$\mathbb{P}(B_s \in \Delta y | B_t \in \Delta x) = A = \frac{\mathbb{P}(B_s \in \Delta y, B_t \in \Delta x)}{\mathbb{P}(B_t \in \Delta x)}$$

The increments of the Brownian Motion being independent we have

$$A = \frac{\mathbb{P}(B_s \in \Delta y)\,\mathbb{P}((B_t - B_s) \in \Delta(y - x))}{\mathbb{P}(B_t \in \Delta x)}$$

$$\mathbb{P}((B_t - B_s) \in \Delta(y - x)) = \frac{1}{\sqrt{2\pi(t - s)}} \exp\left(-\frac{(x - y)^2}{2(t - s)}\right) dx$$

$$A = \frac{1}{\sqrt{2\pi s}} \exp\left(-\frac{y^2}{2s}\right) \frac{1}{\sqrt{2\pi(t - s)}} \exp\left(-\frac{(x - y)^2}{2(t - s)}\right) \sqrt{2\pi t} \exp\left(\frac{x^2}{2t}\right)$$

$$= \frac{\sqrt{t}}{\sqrt{2\pi s(t - s)}} \exp\left(-\frac{(y - \frac{s}{t}x)^2}{\frac{s(t-s)}{t}}\right)$$

We find that B_s is normally distributed with mean $\frac{xs}{t}$ and variance $\frac{s(t-s)}{t}$.

4.9 Martingales? - Solution

Question : Are the following processes martingales?

i) $X_t = B_t + 8t$ iii) $X_t = B_t^3$

ii) $X_t = B_t^2$ iv) $X_t = t^2 B_t - 2\int_0^t sB_s ds$

Solution :

i) $X_t = B_t + 8t$
In this case the expectation is clearly not constant

$$\mathbb{E}(X_t) = \mathbb{E}(B_t) + 8t = 8t$$

Therefore X_t is not a martingale

ii) $X_t = B_t^2$
Again the expectation is not constant

$$\mathbb{E}(B_t^2) = \text{Var}(B_t) - \mathbb{E}(B_t)^2 = t$$

Therefore X_t is not a martingale

iii) $X_t = B_t^3$
In this case the expectation is zero (the distribution function of B_t^3 is even). We can come back to the definition of a martingale, let $t > s$

$$B_t^3 = (B_t - B_s + B_s)^3 = (B_t - B_s)^3 + B_s(B_t - B_s)^2 + B_s^2(B_t - B_s) + B_s^3$$

we take the conditional expectation and we use

$$\mathbb{E}[(B_t - B_s)^3|Fs] = \mathbb{E}[(B_t - B_s)|Fs] = 0$$

and we find

$$\mathbb{E}[B_t^3|Fs] = B_s^3 + (t - s)B_s$$

Therefore X_t is not a martingale

iv) $X_t = t^2 B_t - 2\int_0^t sB_s ds$
We apply Itô on $Y_t = t^2 B_t$

$$dY_t = 2tB_t dt + t^2 dB_t$$

and we find

$$X_t = \int_0^t s^2 dB_s$$

Therefore X_t is a martingale

4.10   Natural Martingale - Solution

Question :   Let Y be a real valued random variable on $(\Omega, \mathcal{F}, P)$ such that

$$E[\|Y\|] < \infty$$

Define

$$M_t = E[Y|\mathcal{F}_t]; \quad t \geq 0$$

Show that M_t is an $\mathcal{F}_t$-martingale. Conversely, let $M_t; t \geq 0$ be a real valued $\mathcal{F}_t$-martingale such that

$$\sup_{t \geq 0} E\left[\|M_t|^p\right] < \infty \quad \text{for some} \quad p > 1$$

Show that there exists $Y \in L^1(P)$ such that $M_t = E[Y|\mathcal{F}_t]$.

Solution :   We prove that M_t is martingale using the tower rule, let $t > s$

$$\mathbb{E}[M_t|\mathcal{F}s] = \mathbb{E}[\mathbb{E}[Y|\mathcal{F}t]|\mathcal{F}s] = \mathbb{E}[Y|\mathcal{F}s] = M_s$$

To prove the existence of Y we use the Doob's Martingale Convergence Theorem (see page 89). M_t is uniformly integrable with the test function $\psi(x) = x^p$, therefore there exists $Y \in L^1(P)$ such that $M_t \to Y$ a.e. (P) and

$$\int |M_t - Y| dP \to 0 \text{ as } t \to \infty$$

therefore for $s > t$

$$\mathbb{E}[Y|\mathcal{F}_t] = \lim_{s \to \infty} \mathbb{E}[M_s|\mathcal{F}_t] = M_t$$

4.11 Exponential Brownian - Solution

Question : Let B_t be Brownian motion on $\mathbf{R}$, $B_0 = 0$. Prove that

$$\mathbb{E}\left[e^{iuB_t}\right] = \exp\left(-\frac{1}{2}u^2 t\right) \qquad \text{for all} \ \ u \in \mathbf{R}$$

Use the power series expansion of the exponential function on both sides, compare the terms with the same power of u and deduce that

$$\mathbb{E}\left[B_t^4\right] = 3t^2$$

and more generally that

$$\mathbb{E}\left[B_t^{2k}\right] = \frac{(2k)!}{2^k \cdot k!} t^k; \quad k \in \mathbf{N}$$

Solution : We use the geometric brownian motion, which we known is a martingale with dynamics $dX_t = \sigma X_t dB_t$

$$\mathbb{E}(X_t) = \mathbb{E}\left(\exp\left(-\frac{1}{2}\sigma^2 t + \sigma B_t\right)\right) = 1$$

and we set $\sigma = iu$ to obtain

$$\mathbb{E}\left[e^{iuB_t}\right] = \exp\left(-\frac{1}{2}u^2 t\right)$$

we use a Taylor expansion on both sides

$$\sum_{i \in \mathbf{N}} \mathbb{E}\left(\frac{(iuB_t)^n}{n!}\right) = \sum_{i \in \mathbf{N}} \frac{(-u^2 t)^n}{2^n n!}$$

The equation above holds for any $u \in \mathbf{R}$, therefore we can identify the terms with the same power of u

$$\mathbb{E}\left(\frac{(iuB_t)^{2n}}{(2n)!}\right) = \frac{(-1)^n (u)^{2n} t^n}{2^n n!}$$

$$\mathbb{E}\left(\frac{u^{2n}(-1)^n (B_t)^{2n}}{(2n)!}\right) = \frac{(-1)^n u^{2n} t^n}{2^n n!}$$

and

$$\mathbb{E}\left(B_t^{2n}\right) = \frac{(2n)!}{2^n n!} t^n$$

Chapter 5

Finance

Finance

5.1 Binary Hedging ♠♠♠ (UBS)

A trader suggests the following binary hedging strategy for a call option:

- sell a call option at strike $K > S_0$
- buy the stock at K when S_t is increasing and crosses K
- sell the stock at K when S_t is decreasing and crosses K

What is wrong with this strategy?

Solution in page 45

5.2 Exchange Option ♠♠ (Credit Suisse)

The payoff of an exchange option at expiry is

$$\text{Ex(T)} = \max \left(S_1(T) - S_2(T)\right)^+$$

Calculate the price of an exchange option at $t = 0$ when ρ is the correlation between S_1 and S_2 and σ and r are constant.

Solution in page 46

5.3 Chooser Option ♠ (Commerzbank)

A chooser option gives the right to choose at some future date τ to receive a call or put option with strike K and final expiry $T > \tau$. The payoff at τ of a standard chooser option is

$$\text{Ch}(\tau) = \max \left(C\left(S_\tau, T - \tau, K\right), P\left(S_\tau, T - \tau, K\right)\right)$$

Calculate the price of a chooser option at $t = 0$ when σ and r are constant.

Solution in page 48

5.4 Forward Start Option ♠ (Goldman sachs)

The terminal payoff of a forward start call option is

$$\text{Fs}(T) = (S_T - KS_{T_0})^+$$

where $0 < T_0 < T$. Calculate the price of a forward start call option at $t = 0$ when σ and r are constant.

Solution in page 48

5.5   Compound Option ♠ (Goldman sachs)

The payoff of a compound option is

$$\text{Co}_{T_0} = (C\,(S_{T_0}, \tau, K) - K_0)^+$$

where $C\,(S_{T_0}, \tau, K)$ stands for the value at time T_0 of a standard call option with strike price K and expiry date $T = T_0 + \tau$. Calculate the price of a compound option at $t = 0$ when σ and r are constant.

Solution in page 49

5.6   At The Money Approximation ♠ (BNP)

Prove the following approximation for the price of an at the money call option

$$C \simeq 0.4 S \sigma \sqrt{T}$$

Solution in page 49

5.7   End of Times ♠♠ (UBS)

Let X_n be a sequence of positive random variables, such that $\mathbb{E}[X_n] = a$ and

$$\lim_{n \to +\infty} X_n = 0 \quad \text{a.s}$$

show that

$$\lim_{n \to +\infty} \mathbb{E}|X_n - K| = a + K$$

Can this result be applied to a financial option?

Solution in page 49

Chapter 6

Finance - Solutions

Finance - Solutions

6.1 Binary Hedging - Solution

Question : A trader suggests the following binary hedging strategy for a call option:

- sell a call option at strike $K > S_0$

- buy the stock at K when S_t is increasing and crosses K

- sell the stock at K when S_t is decreasing and crosses K

What is wrong with this strategy?

Solution : This paradox is more than a simple puzzle. The question is called the stop-go paradox and was discussed in several publications (Seidenverg (1988) Carr (1989) Ingersoll (1987) El Karoui (1978)). Generally many interview candidates invoke transaction costs, liquidity or the impossibility to hit an exact price. But all these answers are incorrect because Black Scholes assumptions allow you to build this portfolio. The second type of answer is usually about the portfolio not being self financing because the trader would need to start with K in cash. This is correct but could be addressed using forward contracts for example. We could also borrow the needed cash and the paradox would still be unsolved if the rates are zero.

The correct short answer is that this portfolio is not continuously derivable at K, this discontinuity can be crossed an infinity of times by the stochastic process, making it not self-financed.

Let us break the paradox mathematically. We construct the portfolio

$$V(t) = -\mathbb{1}_{\{S_t > KP(t)\}} KP(t) + \mathbb{1}_{\{S_t > KP(t)\}} S_t$$

where P(t) is the bond's price. This portfolio replicates the terminal payoff and it must satisfy the following equation for all t in order to be self-financed

$$V(t) = V(0) + \int_0^t m(u)dP(u) + \int_0^t n(u)dS_u$$

For simplicity we take rates constant equal to zero (the general case can be reduced with a change of numeraire). The portfolio is then

$$V(t) = -\mathbb{1}_{\{S_t > K\}} K + \mathbb{1}_{\{S_t > K\}} S_t$$

and the self-financing condition becomes

$$V(t) = V(0) + \int_0^t n(u)dS_u$$

where

$$n(u) = \mathbb{1}_{\{S_u > K\}}$$

the portfolio is self-financed only if the following equation holds

$$V(t) - V(0) \stackrel{?}{=} \int_0^t \mathbb{1}_{\{S_u > K\}} dS_u$$

$$g(S_t) = \mathbb{1}_{\{S_t > K\}}(S_t - K) - (S_0 - K)^+ \stackrel{?}{=} \int_0^t \mathbb{1}_{\{S_u > K\}} dS_u$$

The key here is that g is not C^2 and we cannot apply the usual Itô's lemma, but we can use the Tanaka's formula (see page 90) because g is C^2 outside a finite set of points.

$$g(S_t) = g(S_0) + \int_0^t g'(S_u) dS_u + \lim_{\epsilon \to 0} \frac{1}{2\epsilon} |\{u \in [0, t]; S_u \in [K - \epsilon, K + \epsilon]\}|$$

where g' is the weak derivative of g and $|A|$ is the Lebesgue measure of A. Therefore

$$V(t) - V(0) = \int_0^t \mathbb{1}_{\{S_u > K\}} dS_u + \lim_{\epsilon \to 0} \frac{1}{2\epsilon} |\{u \in [0, t]; S_u \in [K - \epsilon, K + \epsilon]\}|$$

The last term does not converge towards zero and the portfolio is not self-financed, breaking the apparent paradox.

In real business conditions this hedging method is not used because of liquidity and the additional risk associated with this book management method. The delta hedging method is preferred, the trader accepts to pay small regular hedging costs in exchange for a much lower risk.

6.2 Exchange Option - Solution

Question : The payoff of an exchange option at expiry is

$$\text{Ex(T)} = \max \left(S_1(T) - S_2(T) \right)^+$$

Calculate the price of an exchange option at $t = 0$ when ρ is the correlation between S_1 and S_2 and σ and r are constant.

Solution : The dynamics of S_1 and S_2 are given by

$$dS_1(t) = rS_1(t)dt + \sigma_1 S_1(t)dB_1 \ , \ S_1(0) = s_1$$
$$dS_2(t) = rS_2(t)dt + \sigma_2 S_2(t)dB_2 \ , \ S_2(0) = s_2$$

where B_1, B_2 are Brownian motions with $E[dB_1 dB_2] = \rho dt$. We denote C the value of the exchange option at $t = 0$.

$$C = e^{-rt} \mathbb{E}[\max(S_1(T) - S_2(T), 0)]$$
$$= \mathbb{E}\left[\tilde{S}_2(T) \max(S_1(T)/S_2(T) - 1, 0)\right]$$

where $\tilde{S}_i(t) = e^{-rt} S_i(t)$. By the Itô formula, $Y(t) = S_1(t)/S_2(t)$ satisfies

$$dY = Y\left(\sigma_2^2 - \sigma_1\sigma_2\rho\right) dt + Y(\sigma_1 dw_1 - \sigma_2 dw_2)$$

We identify a Girsanov exponential

$$\frac{1}{s_2}\tilde{S}_2(T) = \exp\left(\sigma_2 w_2(T) - \frac{1}{2}\sigma_2^2 T\right)$$

defining a change of measure

$$\frac{d\tilde{P}}{dP} = \frac{1}{s_2}S_2(T)$$

Thus

$$C = s_2\tilde{E}[\max(Y(T) - 1, 0)]$$

By the Girsanov theorem, under measure $\tilde{P}$ the process

$$d\tilde{B}_2 = dB_2 - \sigma_2 dt$$

is a Brownian motion. We can write w_1 as $w_1(t) = \rho w_2(t) + \sqrt{1 - \rho^2}w'(t)$ where $w'(t)$ is a Brownian motion independent of $w_2(t)$ (under measure P). You can check that with $\tilde{P}$ defined above , w' remains a Brownian motion under P, independent of $\tilde{w}_2$. Hence $d\tilde{w}_1$ defined by

$$d\tilde{w}_1 = \rho d\tilde{w}_2(t) + \sqrt{1 - \rho^2}dw'(t)$$
$$= dw_1(t) - \rho\sigma_2 dt$$

is a $\tilde{P}$ -Brownian motion. The equation for Y under $\tilde{P}$ turns out-miraculously-to be

$$dY = Y(\sigma_1 d\tilde{w}_1 - \sigma_2 d\tilde{w}_2)$$

$$dY = Y\sigma dw$$

where w is a standard Brownian motion and σ is given by

$$\sigma = \sqrt{\sigma_1^2 + \sigma_2^2 - 2\rho\sigma_1\sigma_2}$$

We conclude that the exchange option is equivalent to a call option on asset Y with volatility σ, strike 1 and riskless rate 0. By the Black-Scholes formula, this is

$$C(s_1, s_2) = s_1 N(d_1) - s_2 N(d_2)$$

$$d_1 = \frac{\ln(s_1/s_2) + \frac{1}{2}\sigma^2 T}{\sigma\sqrt{T}}$$
$$d_2 = d_1 - \sigma\sqrt{T}$$
$$\sigma = \sqrt{\sigma_1^2 + \sigma_2^2 - 2\rho\sigma_1\sigma_2}$$

6.3   Chooser Option - Solution

Question :   A chooser option gives the right to choose at some future date τ to receive a call or put option with strike K and final expiry $T > \tau$. The payoff at τ of a standard chooser option is

$$\text{Ch}(\tau) = \max\left(C\left(S_\tau, T - \tau, K\right), P\left(S_\tau, T - \tau, K\right)\right)$$

Calculate the price of a chooser option at $t = 0$ when σ and r are constant.

Solution :   Recall that the call-put parity at τ and maturity T implies that

$$P\left(S_\tau, T - \tau, K\right) = C\left(S_\tau, T - \tau, K\right) - S_\tau + Ke^{-r(T-\tau)}$$

We can rewrite the chooser option value at τ

$$\text{Ch}(\tau) = \max\left\{C\left(S_\tau, T - \tau, K\right), C\left(S_\tau, T - \tau, K\right) - S_\tau + Ke^{-r(T-\tau)}\right\}$$

or finally

$$\text{Ch}(\tau) = C\left(S_\tau, T - \tau, K\right) + \left(Ke^{-r(T-\tau)} - S_\tau\right)^+$$

The last equality implies immediately that the standard chooser option is equivalent to the portfolio composed of a long call option and a long put option (with different exercise prices and different expiry dates), so that its arbitrage price equals, for every $t \in [0, \tau]$,

$$\text{Ch}(t) = C\left(S_t, T - t, K\right) + P\left(S_t, \tau - t, Ke^{-r(T-\tau)}\right)$$

In particular, using the Black-Scholes formula, we get for $t = 0$

$$\text{Ch}(0) = S_0\left(N\left(d_1\right) - N\left(-\bar{d}_1\right)\right) + Ke^{-rT}\left(N\left(-\bar{d}_2\right) - N\left(d_2\right)\right)$$

where

$$d_{1,2} = \frac{\ln\left(S_0/K\right) + \left(r \pm \frac{1}{2}\sigma^2\right)T}{\sigma\sqrt{T}}$$

and

$$\bar{d}_{1,2} = \frac{\ln\left(S_0/K\right) + rT \pm \frac{1}{2}\sigma^2\tau}{\sigma\sqrt{\tau}}$$

6.4   Forward Start Option - Solution

Question :   The terminal payoff of a forward start call option is

$$\text{Fs}(T) = \left(S_T - KS_{T_0}\right)^+$$

where $0 < T_0 < T$. Calculate the price of a forward start call option at $t = 0$ when σ and r are constant.

Solution :   Let us consider the case of a forward-start call option, with terminal payoff

$$\text{Fs}(T) = \left(S_T - KS_{T_0}\right)^+$$

To find the price at time $t \in [0, T_0]$ of such an option, it suffices to consider its value at the delivery date T_0, that is, the price at time T_0 of the at-the-money option with expiry date T. Thus, we have

$$Fs(T_0) = C(S_{T_0}, T - T_0, KS_{T_0})$$

Where $C(S, T, K)$ is the price of call option with spot S, time to expiry $(T - T_0)$ and strike K. We can factor S_{T_0} and divide the spot and the strike

$$C(S_{T_0}, T - T_0, KS_{T_0}) = S_{T_0} C(1, T - T_0, K)$$

since $C(1, T - T_0, K)$ is non-random, the option's value at time 0 equals

$$Fs(T_0) = \mathbb{E}_0(S_{T_0}) \exp(-rT_0) C(1, T - T_0, K) = C(S_0, T - T_0, S_0 K)$$

$$Fs(T_0) = S_0 C(1, T - T_0, K) = C(S_0, T - T_0, S_0 K)$$

Note that the Forward Start Option has a closed formula when σ is constant, but its pricing becomes much more complex when the volatility surface is not trivial. Forward Start Option are notoriously sensitive to the forward skew and require a specific model, for example a stochastic volatility model.

6.5   Compound Option - Solution

Question :   The payoff of a compound option is

$$Co_{T_0} = (C(S_{T_0}, \tau, K) - K_0)^+$$

where $C(S_{T_0}, \tau, K)$ stands for the value at time T_0 of a standard call option with strike price K and expiry date $T = T_0 + \tau$. Calculate the price of a compound option at $t = 0$ when σ and r are constant.

Solution :   There is no simple closed formula for Compound Option, the final result will be an integral. We start with the price of a call option

$$C(s, \tau, K) = sN(d_1(s, \tau, K)) - Ke^{-r\tau} N(d_2(s, \tau, K))$$

Moreover, since under $\mathbb{P}^*$ we have

$$S_{T_0} = S_0 \exp\left(\sigma\sqrt{T_0}\xi + \left(r - \frac{1}{2}\sigma^2\right) T_0\right)$$

where ξ has a standard Gaussian probability law under $\mathbb{P}^*$, the price of the compound option at time 0 equals

$$Co_0 = e^{-rT_0} \int_{x_0}^{\infty} \left(g(x)N(\hat{d}_1) - Ke^{-r\tau} N(\hat{d}_2) - K_0\right) n(x) dx$$

where $\hat{d}_i = d_i(g(x), \tau, K)$ for $i = 1, 2$, n is the density of the standard normal distribution, the function $g : \mathbb{R} \to \mathbb{R}$ is given by the formula

$$g(x) = S_0 \exp\left(\sigma\sqrt{T_0}x + \left(r - \frac{1}{2}\sigma^2\right) T_0\right)$$

and, finally, the constant x_0 is defined implicitly by the equation

$$x_0 = \inf\{x \in \mathbb{R} | C(g(x), \tau, K) \geq K_0\}$$

Straightforward calculations yield

$$d_1(g(x), \tau, K) = \frac{\ln(S_0/K) + \sigma\sqrt{T_0}x + rT - \sigma^2 T_0 + \frac{1}{2}\sigma^2 T}{\sigma\sqrt{T - T_0}}$$

and

$$d_2(g(x), \tau, K) = \frac{\ln(S_0/K) + \sigma\sqrt{T_0}x + rT - \frac{1}{2}\sigma^2 T}{\sigma\sqrt{T - T_0}}$$

6.6 At The Money Approximation - Solution

Question : Prove the following approximation for the price of an at the money call option

$$C \simeq 0.4S\sigma\sqrt{T}$$

Solution : We start with the call option price formula

$$C = S\phi(d_1) - Ke^{-rT}\phi(d_2)$$

where

$$d_1 = \frac{\ln\left(\frac{S_0}{K}\right) + rT + \frac{\sigma^2 T}{2}}{\sigma\sqrt{T}} \quad , \quad d_2 = \frac{\ln\left(\frac{S_0}{K}\right) + rT - \frac{\sigma^2 T}{2}}{\sigma\sqrt{T}}$$

the call is at the money so

$$C = S\left(\phi(d_1) - \phi(d_2)\right)$$

where

$$d_1 = \frac{\sigma\sqrt{T}}{2} \quad , \quad d_2 = \frac{-\sigma\sqrt{T}}{2}$$

and

$$\phi(d_1) - \phi(d_2) = \int_{d_2}^{d_1} n(x)dx$$

where n is the density function of the standard normal distribution. Now the volatility is usually below 0.5, and for relatively short expiries (less than 2 years) we can approximate the integral with the area of a rectangle

$$\int_{d_2}^{d_1} n(x)dx \simeq 2n(0)d_1 \simeq 0.4\sigma\sqrt{T}$$

and

$$C \simeq 0.4S\sigma\sqrt{T}$$

6.7   End of Times - Solution

Question :   Let X_n be a sequence of positive random variables, such that $\mathbb{E}[X_n] = a$ and

$$\lim_{n \to +\infty} X_n = 0 \quad \text{a.s}$$

show that

$$\lim_{n \to +\infty} \mathbb{E}|X_n - K| = a + K$$

Can this result be applied to a financial option?

Solution :   To solve elegantly this question, a formula to remember is

$$|X_n - K| = X_n + K - 2\min(Xn, K)$$

X_n converges a.s towards 0, therefore $\mathbb{E}[\min(Xn, K)]$ converges towards 0 too. So

$$lim_{n \to +\infty} E(|X_n - K|) = lim_{n \to +\infty} \mathbb{E}[X_n] + K = a + K$$

The financial option we can associate with this result is a straddle with payoff

$$\text{Payoff}_T = |S_T - K|$$

At the money forward the price becomes

$$P = \mathbb{E}\left[\exp(-rT)|S_T - K|\right] = \mathbb{E}\left[|\exp(-rT)S_T - S_0|\right]$$

$$P = \mathbb{E}\left[|S_0 Y_T - S_0|\right]$$

where

$$Y_T = \exp\left(\sigma\sqrt{T}\xi - \frac{1}{2}\sigma^2 T\right)$$

with ξ a standard normal variable. Now let A be a real number, we have

$$P\left(\sigma\sqrt{T}\xi - \frac{1}{2}\sigma^2 T > A\right) = P\left(\xi > \frac{A}{\sigma\sqrt{T}} + \frac{\sigma\sqrt{T}}{2}\right)$$

We see that if $\sigma \to +\infty$ or $T \to +\infty$, $\left(\sigma\sqrt{T}\xi - \frac{1}{2}\sigma^2 T\right) \to +\infty$ a.s and $Y_n \to 0$ a.s. Using the previous result, we conclude that the price of the at the money forward straddle price converges towards $2S_0$ when the maturity is very long or the volatility very high.

Chapter 7

Programming

Programming

7.1 Best Sort ♠♠ (Hedge Fund)

For a comparison sort (where nothing is assumed about the items except that they can be compared), what is the best complexity?

Prove that this is the tightest bound.

Solution in page 59

7.2 Merge Sort ♠ (Citi)

Write a code for merge sort in the language of your choice or pseudo code.

Solution in page 59

7.3 Quick Sort ♠ (Citi)

Write a code for quick sort in the language of your choice or pseudo language.

Solution in page 60

7.4 Struct vs Class ♠ (Credit Suisse)

how does a struct differ from a class in C++ ?

Solution in page 61

7.5 Friend Class ♠ (Credit Suisse)

What is a friend class in C++ ?

Solution in page 61

7.6 Singleton ♠♠♠ (Goldman Sachs)

Explain C++ Singleton design pattern. Implement a version in C++ .

Solution in page 61

7.7 Is Python Compiled? ♠♠ (Goldman Sachs)

Is python a compiled language?

Solution in page 63

7.8 Python Hash ♠♠ (Goldman Sachs)

How is the hash function used in python?

Solution in page 63

7.9 Python Self ♠♠ (Hedge Fund)

Explain the keyword self in python.

Solution in page 64

Chapter 8

Programming - Solutions

Programming - Solutions

8.1 Best Sort - Solution

Question : For a comparison sort (where nothing is assumed about the items except that they can be compared), what is the best complexity?
Prove that this is the tightest bound.

Solution : The best complexity in this case is $\mathcal{O}(N \log(N))$. Let N be the number of elements in the list. There are N possible permutations of the list. Sorting the list is equivalent to discovering which of these permutations sorts the list. By symmetry a given comparison eliminates half of the remaining permutations, because the number of permutations where a_i is after a_j is equal to the number of permutations where a_j is after a_i. Therefore the best complexity T satisfies

$$\frac{N!}{2^T} = 1$$

and

$$T = \frac{\log(N!)}{\log(2)}$$

Note that $\log(N!) \simeq N \log(N)$, we can prove it with the Sterling formula, or by decomposing the log and seeing a Riemann integral

$$\log(N!) = \log(2) + \log(3) + \cdots + \log(N) \simeq \int_1^N \log(u)du = N \log(N) - N$$

Therefore the best complexity is the highest order and

$$T \simeq \mathcal{O}(N \log(N))$$

8.2 Merge Sort - Solution

Question : Write a code for merge sort in the language of your choice or pseudo code.

Solution : Our advice for this type of question is to use python. If you choose C++ you will make the task longer and if you choose pseudo code you will most likely raise questions about which subfunctions you assumed to be available. By using python you will write short code and tick the python box with the interviewer.

```
# Python program for implementation of MergeSort
def mergeSort(arr):
    if len(arr) >1:
        mid = len(arr)//2 # Finding the mid of the array
        L = arr[:mid] # Dividing the array elements
        R = arr[mid:] # into 2 halves

        mergeSort(L) # Sorting the first half
        mergeSort(R) # Sorting the second half
```

```
i = j = k = 0

# Copy data to temp arrays L[] and R[]
while i < len(L) and j < len(R):
    if L[i] < R[j]:
        arr[k] = L[i]
        i+= 1
    else:
        arr[k] = R[j]
        j+= 1
    k+= 1

# Checking if any element was left
while i < len(L):
    arr[k] = L[i]
    i+= 1
    k+= 1

while j < len(R):
    arr[k] = R[j]
    j+= 1
    k+= 1
```

8.3   Quick Sort - Solution

Question :   Write a code for quick sort in the language of your choice or pseudo language.

Solution :

```
# Python program for implementation of Quicksort Sort
# This function takes last element as pivot, places
# the pivot element at its correct position in sorted
# array, and places all smaller (smaller than pivot)
# to left of pivot and all greater elements to right
# of pivot
def partition(arr, low, high):
    i = ( low-1 )          # index of smaller element
    pivot = arr[high]      # pivot

    for j in range(low , high):

        # If current element is smaller than or
        # equal to pivot
        if   arr[j] <= pivot:

            # increment index of smaller element
            i = i+1
            arr[i], arr[j] = arr[j], arr[i]
```

```
arr[i+1], arr[high] = arr[high], arr[i+1]
return ( i+1 )
```

```
# The main function that implements QuickSort
# arr[] ---> Array to be sorted,
# low    ---> Starting index,
# high   ---> Ending index

# Util Function to do Quick sort
def quickSort_Util(arr, low, high):
    if low < high:

        # pi is partitioning index, arr[p] is now
        # at right place
        pi = partition(arr, low, high)

        # Separately sort elements before
        # partition and after partition
        quickSort_Util(arr, low, pi-1)
        quickSort_Util(arr, pi+1, high)

# Main Function to do Quick sort
def quickSort(arr):
    quickSort_Util(arr, 0, len(arr)-1)
```

8.4 Struct vs Class - Solution

Question : how does a struct differ from a class in C++ ?

Solution : The only difference between a struct and class in C++ is the default accessibility of member variables and methods. In a struct they are public; in a class they are private.

8.5 Friend Class - Solution

Question : What is a friend class in C++ ?

Solution : A friend class can access private and protected members of other class in which it is declared as friend. It is sometimes useful to allow a particular class to access private members of other class.

8.6 Singleton - Solution

Question : Explain C++ Singleton design pattern. Implement a version in C++ .

Solution : Singleton design pattern is a software design principle that is used to restrict the instantiation of a class to one object. This is useful when exactly one object is needed to coordinate actions across the system. For example, if you are using a logger, that writes logs to a file, you can use a singleton class to create such a logger. You can create a singleton class using the following code

```cpp
#include <iostream>

using namespace std;

class Singleton {
    static Singleton *instance;
    int data;

    // Private constructor so that no objects can be created.
    Singleton() {
        data = 0;
    }

    public:
    static Singleton *getInstance() {
        if (!instance)
        instance = new Singleton;
        return instance;
    }

    int getData() {
        return this -> data;
    }

    void setData(int data) {
        this -> data = data;
    }
};

//Initialize pointer to zero so that it can be initialized
//in first call to getInstance
Singleton *Singleton :: instance = 0;

int main(){
    Singleton *s = s->getInstance();
    cout << s->getData() << endl;
    s->setData(100);
    cout << s->getData() << endl;
    return 0;
}
```

This will give the output

0
100

8.7 Is Python Compiled? - Solution

Question :   Is python a compiled language?

Solution :   This is a common question. Usually, "compile" means to convert a program in a high-level language into a binary executable full of machine code (CPU instructions). In Python, the source code is compiled into a much simpler form called bytecode. These are instructions similar in spirit to CPU instructions, but instead of being executed by the CPU, they are executed by software called a virtual machine. So the answer is Python is not directly compiled to CPU instructions, but it is still compiled to virtual machine language.

8.8   Python Hash - Solution

Question :   How is the hash function used in python?

Solution :   Hash tables are used to implement map and set data structures in many common programming languages, such as C++ , Java, and Python. Python uses hash tables for dictionaries and sets. A hash table is an unordered collection of key-value pairs, where each key is unique. Hash tables offer a combination of efficient lookup, insert and delete operations. These are the best properties of arrays and linked lists.

Hashing is the process of using an algorithm to map data of any size to a fixed length. This is called a hash value. Hashing is used to create high performance, direct access data structures where large amount of data is to be stored and accessed quickly. Hash values are computed with hash functions.

An object is hashable if it has a hash value which never changes during its lifetime. (It can have different values during multiple invocations of Python programs.) A hashable object needs a ___hash___() method. In order to perform comparisons, a hashable needs an ___eq___() method.

Note: Hashable objects which compare equal must have the same hash value. Hashability makes an object usable as a dictionary key and a set member, because these data structures use the hash value internally. Python immutable built-in objects are hashable; mutable containers (such as lists or dictionaries) are not. Objects which are instances of user-defined classes are hashable by default. They all compare unequal (except with themselves), and their hash value is derived from their id().

Note: If a class does not define an ___eq___() method it should not define a ___hash___() operation either; if it defines ___eq___() but not ___hash___(), its instances will not be usable as items in hashable collections. Python hash() function The hash() function returns the hash value of the object if it has one. Hash values are integers. They are used to quickly compare dictionary keys during a dictionary lookup. Objects can implement the ___hash___() method.

Python immutable builtins, such as integers, strings, or tuples, are hashable. Below a class implementation with a hash function.

```python
class User:

    def __init__(self, name, job):
```

```
        self.name = name
        self.job = job

    def __eq__(self, other):

        return self.name == other.name \
            and self.job == other.job

    def __str__(self):
        return f'{self.name} {self.job}'
```

8.9 Python Self - Solution

Question :   Explain the keyword self in python.

Solution :
self represents the instance of the class. By using the "self" keyword we can access the attributes and methods of the class in python. It binds the attributes with the given arguments.

The reason you need to use self is because Python does not use the @ syntax to refer to instance attributes. Python decided to do methods in a way that makes the instance to which the method belongs be passed automatically, but not received automatically: the first parameter of methods is the instance the method is called on.

```
class car():

    # init method or constructor
    def __init__(self, model, color):
        self.make = make
        self.color = color

    def show(self):
        print("make is", self.make )
        print("color is", self.color )

# both objects have different self which
# contain their attributes
audi = car("audi", "blue")
ferrari = car("ferrari", "green")

audi.show()      # same output as car.show(audi)
ferrari.show()   # same output as car.show(ferrari)

# Behind the scene, in every instance method
# call, python sends the instances also with
# that method call like car.show(audi)
```

self is parameter in function and user can use another parameter name in place of it.But it is advisable to use self because it increase the readability of code.

Chapter 9

Classic Calculations

Classic Calculations

9.1 Call Option ♠♠ (Societe Generale)

Derive the formula for the price of a call option using Girsanov theorem.

Solution in page 71

9.2 Greeks ♠♠ (Societe Generale)

Calculate the greeks Δ, Γ, $\mathcal{V}$, ρ, Θ for a call option.

Solution in page 72

9.3 Ornstein Uhlenbeck ♠♠ (JP Morgan)

Derive the formula of an Ornstein Uhlenbeck process. Calculate its expectation and variance.

Solution in page 74

9.4 Hybrid Vasicek ♠♠♠ (JP Morgan)

Derive the relationship between the stock volatility and the rates volatility in a hybrid Vasicek model.

Solution in page 75

9.5 Fokker-Planck ♠♠♠ (Morgan Stanley)

Derive the Fokker-Planck formula.

Solution in page 76

9.6 Breeden-Litzenberger ♠♠♠ (Morgan Stanley)

Derive the Breeden-Litzenberger Formula.

Solution in page 78

9.7 Local Volatility ♠♠♠ (Morgan Stanley)

Derive the Dupire Formula or Local Volatility.

Solution in page 79

9.8 Black Scholes Equation ♠♣ (BNP)

Derive the Black Scholes equation.

Solution in page 80

Chapter 10

Classic Calculations - Solutions

Classic Calculations - Solutions

10.1   Call Option - Solution

Question :   Derive the formula for the price of a call option using Girsanov theorem.

Solution :   We denote C the price at $t = 0$ of a call option.

$$C = e^{-rT}\mathbb{E}(S_T - K)^+ = e^{-rT}\mathbb{E}\left(S_T 1_{(S_T \geq K)} - K 1_{(S_T \geq K)}\right)$$

Where S_t is the process

$$S_t = S_0 exp\left(rt - \frac{\sigma^2 t}{2} + \sigma W_t\right)$$

We decompose $C = A - B$ and start calculating the second term B

$$B = e^{-rT}K\mathbb{E}\left(1_{(S_T \geq K)}\right) = e^{-rT}KP(S_T \geq K)$$

$$B = e^{-rT}KP\left(ln\left(\frac{S_0}{K}\right) + rT - \frac{\sigma^2 T}{2} + \sigma W_T \geq 0\right)$$

$$B = e^{-rT}KP\left(W_T \geq \frac{ln\left(\frac{K}{S_0}\right) - rT + \frac{\sigma^2 T}{2}}{\sigma}\right)$$

$$B = e^{-rT}KP\left(W_T \leq \frac{ln\left(\frac{S_0}{K}\right) + rT - \frac{\sigma^2 T}{2}}{\sigma}\right)$$

$$B = e^{-rT}KP\left(X \leq \frac{ln\left(\frac{S_0}{K}\right) + rT - \frac{\sigma^2 T}{2}}{\sigma\sqrt{T}}\right) = Ke^{-rT}\phi(d_2)$$

where $X \sim \mathcal{N}(0,1)$ and ϕ is the standard cumulative normal distribution. The calculation for A is trickier

$$A = e^{-rT}\mathbb{E}\left(S_T 1_{(S_T \geq K)}\right) = S_0\mathbb{E}\left(exp\left(-\frac{\sigma^2 t}{2} + \sigma W_t\right)1_{(S_T \geq K)}\right)$$

We identify a Girsanov change of measure where

$$Q(E) = \int_E Z_t dP$$

and

$$Z_t = exp\left(\int_0^t \sigma dW s - \int_0^t \frac{\sigma^2}{2} ds\right)$$

$$A = S_0 Q\big(S_T \geq K\big)$$

In this new measure $\hat{W}_t$ is a Brownian Motion where

$$\hat{W}_t = W_t - \int_0^t \sigma ds$$

Therefore the dynamics of S_t in the new measure are

$$S_t = S_0 exp\left(rt + \frac{\sigma^2 t}{2} + \sigma \hat{W}_t\right)$$

$$A = S_0 Q\left(X \leq \frac{ln\left(\frac{S_0}{K}\right) + rT + \frac{\sigma^2 T}{2}}{\sigma\sqrt{T}}\right) = S_0 \phi(d_1)$$

We combine them to find the price of the call option

$$C = S_0 \phi(d_1) - K e^{-rT} \phi(d_2)$$

where

$$d_1 = \frac{ln\left(\frac{S_0}{K}\right) + rT + \frac{\sigma^2 T}{2}}{\sigma\sqrt{T}} \;,\; d_2 = \frac{ln\left(\frac{S_0}{K}\right) + rT - \frac{\sigma^2 T}{2}}{\sigma\sqrt{T}}$$

Note that with dividends the formula becomes

$$C = S_0 e^{-qT} \phi(d_1) - K e^{-rT} \phi(d_2)$$

$$d_1 = \frac{ln\left(\frac{S_0}{K}\right) + (r-q)T + \frac{\sigma^2 T}{2}}{\sigma\sqrt{T}} \;,\; d_2 = \frac{ln\left(\frac{S_0}{K}\right) + (r-q)T - \frac{\sigma^2 T}{2}}{\sigma\sqrt{T}}$$

Sometimes a different formula can be found using the forward $F = S_0 e^{(r-q)T}$

$$C = F e^{-rT} \phi(d_1) - K e^{-rT} \phi(d_2)$$

$$d_1 = \frac{ln\left(\frac{F}{K}\right) + \frac{\sigma^2 T}{2}}{\sigma\sqrt{T}} \;,\; d_2 = \frac{ln\left(\frac{F}{K}\right) - \frac{\sigma^2 T}{2}}{\sigma\sqrt{T}}$$

and the put option price can be derived similarly

$$P = K e^{-rT} \phi(-d_2) - F e^{-rT} \phi(-d_1)$$

10.2   Greeks - Solution

Question :   Calculate the greeks Δ, Γ, $\mathcal{V}$, ρ, Θ for a call option.

Solution :   We denote C the price of the call option at $t = 0$, ϕ the standard normal cumulative distribution and $f = \phi'$ the standard normal density function.

$$C = S_0 \phi(d_1) - K e^{-rT} \phi(d_2)$$

$$d_1 = \frac{ln\left(\frac{S_0}{K}\right) + rT + \frac{\sigma^2 T}{2}}{\sigma\sqrt{T}} \;,\; d_2 = \frac{ln\left(\frac{S_0}{K}\right) + rT - \frac{\sigma^2 T}{2}}{\sigma\sqrt{T}} = d_1 - \sigma\sqrt{T}$$

We start with an identity that will help us for all the greeks

$$f(d_2) = \frac{1}{\sqrt{2\pi}} \exp\left(\frac{-d_2^2}{2}\right) = \frac{1}{\sqrt{2\pi}} \exp\left(\frac{-d_1^2}{2}\right) \exp\left(d_1\sigma\sqrt{T}\right) \exp\left(\frac{-\sigma^2 T}{2}\right)$$

$$f(d_2) = \frac{1}{\sqrt{2\pi}} \exp\left(\frac{-d_1^2}{2}\right) \frac{S_0}{K} \exp(rT) = f(d_1)\frac{S_0}{K}e^{rT} \qquad (3)$$

- Δ

$$\Delta = \frac{\partial C}{\partial S_0} = \phi(d_1) + S_0 f(d_1)\frac{\partial d_1}{\partial S_0} - Ke^{-rT} f(d_2)\frac{\partial d_2}{\partial S_0}$$

$$\Delta = \phi(d_1) + f(d_1)\frac{1}{\sigma\sqrt{T}} - Ke^{-rT} f(d_2)\frac{S_0}{\sigma\sqrt{T}}$$

And using the equation 3

$$\Delta = \phi(d_1)$$

- Γ

$$\Gamma = f(d_1)\frac{1}{S_0\sigma\sqrt{T}}$$

- $\mathcal{V}$

$$\mathcal{V} = \frac{\partial C}{\partial \sigma} = S_0 f(d_1)\frac{\partial d_1}{\partial \sigma} - Ke^{-rT} f(d_2)\frac{\partial d_2}{\partial \sigma}$$

$$\mathcal{V} = \frac{\partial C}{\partial \sigma} = S_0 f(d_1)\frac{\partial d_1}{\partial \sigma} - Ke^{-rT} f(d_2)\left(\frac{\partial d_1}{\partial \sigma} - \sqrt{T}\right)$$

And using equation 3

$$\mathcal{V} = Ke^{-rT} f(d_2)\sqrt{T} = S_0 f(d_1)\sqrt{T}$$

- ρ

$$\rho = \frac{\partial C}{\partial r} = S_0 f(d_1)\frac{\partial d_1}{\partial r} + TKe^{-rT}\phi(d_2) - Ke^{-rT} f(d_2)\frac{\partial d_2}{\partial r}$$

$$\rho = S_0 f(d_1)\frac{\sqrt{T}}{\sigma} + TKe^{-rT}\phi(d_2) - Ke^{-rT} f(d_2)\frac{\sqrt{T}}{\sigma}$$

And using equation 3

$$\rho = TKe^{-rT}\phi(d_2)$$

- Θ

$$\Theta = \frac{\partial C}{\partial T} = S_0 f(d_1)\frac{\partial d_1}{\partial T} + rKe^{-rT}\phi(d_2) - Ke^{-rT} f(d_2)\frac{\partial d_2}{\partial T}$$

$$\Theta = S_0 f(d_1)\frac{\partial d_1}{\partial T} + rKe^{-rT}\phi(d_2) - Ke^{-rT} f(d_2)\left(\frac{\partial d_1}{\partial T} - \frac{\sigma}{2\sqrt{T}}\right)$$

And using equation 3

$$\Theta = rKe^{-rT}\phi(d_2) + Ke^{-rT} f(d_2)\frac{\sigma}{2\sqrt{T}}$$

10.3 Ornsetin Uhlenbeck - Solution

Question : Derive the formula of an Ornstein Uhlenbeck process. Calculate its expectation and variance.

Solution : We start with the dynamics of an Ornsetin Uhlenbeck process

$$dr_t = \theta(\mu - r_t)\,dt + \sigma dW_t$$

We consider the process $X_t = e^{At}r_t$. We apply Itô

$$dX_t = Ae^{At}r_t dt + e^{At}dr_t$$

We find that the value $A = \theta$ gives

$$dX_t = e^{\theta t}(\theta\mu dt + \sigma dW_t)$$

$$X_T - X_0 = \int_0^T \theta\mu e^{\theta t}dt + \int_0^T \sigma e^{\theta t}dW_t$$

$$r_T e^{\theta T} = r_0 + \mu(e^{\theta T} - 1) + \int_0^T \sigma e^{\theta t}dW_t$$

$$r_T = r_0 e^{-\theta T} + \mu(1 - e^{-\theta T}) + \int_0^T \sigma e^{\theta(t-T)}dW_t$$

We find that the expectation is

$$\mathbb{E}(r_T) = r_0 e^{-\theta T} + \mu(1 - e^{-\theta T})$$

and

$$\lim_{T\to\infty} \mathbb{E}(r_T) = \mu$$

We eliminate the deterministic terms for the variance, we find that

$$\text{Var}(r_T) = \text{Var}\left(\int_0^T \sigma e^{\theta(t-T)}dW_t\right)$$

$$\text{Var}(r_T) = \mathbb{E}\left(\left(\int_0^T \sigma e^{\theta(t-T)}dW_t\right)^2\right)$$

We apply the Itô isometry

$$\text{Var}(r_T) = \int_0^T \sigma^2 e^{2\theta(t-T)}dt$$

$$\text{Var}(r_T) = \frac{\sigma^2}{2\theta}(1 - e^{-2\theta T})$$

and

$$\lim_{T\to\infty} \text{Var}(r_T) = \frac{\sigma^2}{2\theta}$$

10.4   Hybrid Vasicek - Solution

Question :   Derive the relationship between the stock volatility and the rates volatility in a hybrid Vasicek model.

Solution :   The interviewer is asking you to derive the classic calibration formula for equity model with stochastic rates. We consider the stock dynamics

$$\frac{\mathrm{d}S_t}{S_t} = r_t\mathrm{dt} + \sigma_t^S\mathrm{d}W_t^S$$

where r_t follows

$$\mathrm{d}r_t = (\theta_t - \kappa r_t)\,\mathrm{d}t + \sigma_t^r\mathrm{d}W_t^r$$

Using the Ornstein Uhlenbeck derivation in the previous question we have

$$r_s = \int_t^s \exp(\kappa(u-s))\sigma_u^r\mathrm{d}W_u + \text{nonstochastic terms}$$

Therefore S_T can be written

$$S_T = S_tP(t,T)exp\left(-\int_t^T \frac{\sigma_u^{s\,2}u}{2}\mathrm{du} + \int_t^T \sigma_u^sW_u^s\mathrm{du}\right)$$

where

$$P(t,T) = \mathbb{E}^{\mathrm{P}}\left[\exp\left(-\int_t^T r_s\mathrm{ds}\right)\right]$$

$$= \mathbb{E}^{\mathrm{P}}\left[\exp\left(-\int_t^T\int_t^s \exp(\kappa(u-s))\sigma_u^r\mathrm{d}W_u^r\mathrm{ds}\right)\right]$$

In order to process this integral we notice that

$$\int_t^T\int_t^s F(u,s)\mathrm{duds} = \int_t^T\int_s^T F(u,s)\mathrm{dsdu}$$

When applied in this case we obtain

$$P(t,T) = \mathbb{E}^{\mathrm{P}}\left[\exp\left(-\int_t^T \hat{B}(\kappa,u,T)\sigma_u^r\mathrm{d}W_u^r\right)\right]$$

where

$$\hat{B}(\kappa,u,T) = \frac{1 - \exp(\kappa(u-T))}{\kappa}$$

We have found the volatility of the zero-coupon bond. We can find the drift using the fact that $P(t,T)$ is tradable, so $P(t,T)/B_t$ must be a $\mathbb{P}$-martingale and so we have

$$\frac{\mathrm{d}P(t,T)}{P(t,T)} = r_t\mathrm{dt} - \hat{B}(\kappa,t,T)\sigma_t^r\mathrm{d}W_t^r$$

Since S_t is tradable, $S_t/P(t,T)$ will be a $\mathbb{Q}_T$-martingale, so it follows that

$$\frac{d\left(\frac{X_t}{P(t,T)}\right)}{\frac{X_t}{P(t,T)}} = \sigma_t^S d\widetilde{W}_t^S + \hat{B}(\kappa,t,T)\sigma_t^r d\widetilde{W}_t^r$$

where $\widetilde{W}_t$ are Brownian motions in $\mathbb{Q}_T$. It follows that under $\mathbb{Q}_T$, S_T is log-normally distributed with mean $S_0/P(0,T)$ and variance

$$V_T = \int_0^T \left(\left(\sigma_t^S\right)^2 + 2\rho\sigma_t^S \hat{B}(\kappa,t,T)\sigma_t^r + \hat{B}(\kappa,t,T)^2 \left(\sigma_t^r\right)^2\right) dt$$

Now we calibrate the hybrid model to the market equity implied volatility by ensuring that

$$\sigma_{\text{imp}}^2(T) = \frac{1}{T}\int_0^T \left(\left(\sigma_t^S\right)^2 + 2\rho\sigma_t^S \hat{B}(\kappa,t,T)\sigma_t^r + \hat{B}(\kappa,t,T)^2 \left(\sigma_t^r\right)^2\right) dt$$

Calibrating here means deriving σ_t^S. σ_{imp} is the market implied volatility (deduced from equity vanilla options prices) and σ_t^r is the rates market implied volatility.

10.5 Fokker-Planck - Solution

Question : Derive the Fokker-Planck formula.

Solution :
Start with the SDE defined by

$$dX_t = \mu\left(X_t\right)dt + \sigma\left(X_t\right)dW_t$$

the transition density $\rho(x,t|y,s)$ is defined by

$$\int_A \rho(x,t|y,s)dx = \Pr\left[X_{t+s} \in A|X_s = y\right]$$
$$= \Pr\left[X_t \in A|X_0 = y\right]$$

Consider a differentiable function $V\left(X_t,t\right) = V(x,t)$ with $V\left(X_t,t\right) = 0$ for $t \notin (0,T)$. Then by Itô's Lemma

$$dV = \left[\frac{\partial V}{\partial t} + \mu\frac{\partial V}{\partial x} + \frac{1}{2}\sigma^2\frac{\partial^2 V}{\partial x^2}\right]dt + \left[\sigma\frac{\partial V}{\partial x}\right]dW_t$$

so that

$$V\left(X_T,T\right) - V\left(X_0,0\right) = \int_0^T \left[\frac{\partial V}{\partial t} + \mu\frac{\partial V}{\partial x} + \frac{1}{2}\sigma^2\frac{\partial^2 V}{\partial x^2}\right]dt + \int_0^T \left[\sigma\frac{\partial V}{\partial x}\right]dW_t \quad (4)$$

where $\mu = \mu\left(X_t\right)$ and $\sigma = \sigma\left(X_t\right)$ for notational convenience. Take the conditional expectation of both sides of equation (4) given X_0

$$E\left[V\left(X_T,T\right) - V\left(X_0,0\right)\right]$$

$$= E\int_0^T \left[\frac{\partial V}{\partial t} + \mu\frac{\partial V}{\partial x} + \frac{1}{2}\sigma^2\frac{\partial^2 V}{\partial x^2}\right]dt + E\int_0^T \left[\sigma\frac{\partial V}{\partial x}\right]dW_t \quad (5)$$

$$= \int_{\mathbb{R}} \left\{ \int_0^T \left[\frac{\partial V}{\partial t} + \mu \frac{\partial V}{\partial x} + \frac{1}{2} \sigma^2 \frac{\partial^2 V}{\partial x^2} \right] dt \right\} \rho(x,t \mid y, s) dx$$

all expectations are expectations conditional on X_0, so that $E[\cdot] = E[\cdot \mid X_0 = y]$. since $E[dW_t] = 0$, the second term in the middle line of equation (5) drops out. Hence, we can write equation (5) as three integrals

$$\int_{\mathbb{R}} \int_0^T \rho \frac{\partial V}{\partial t} dt dx + \int_{\mathbb{R}} \int_0^T \rho \mu \frac{\partial V}{\partial x} dt dx + \frac{1}{2} \int_{\mathbb{R}} \int_0^T \rho \sigma^2 \frac{\partial^2 V}{\partial x^2} dt dx = I_1 + I_2 + I_3 \quad (6)$$

where $\rho = \rho(x, t \mid y, s)$ for notational convenience. The objective of the derivation is to apply integration by parts to get rid of the derivatives of V. The trick is that I_1 is evaluated using integration by parts on t, while I_2 and I_3 are each evaluated using integration by parts on x.

Use $u = \rho$, $v' = \frac{\partial V}{\partial t}$ so that $u' = \frac{\partial \rho}{\partial t}$ and $v = V$. Hence for the inside integrand of I_1 we have

$$\int_0^T \rho \frac{\partial V}{\partial t} dt = \rho V \big|_0^T - \int_0^T \frac{\partial \rho}{\partial t} V dt = - \int_0^T \frac{\partial \rho}{\partial t} V dt$$

since at the boundaries 0 and T, $V = 0$. Hence

$$I_1 = - \int_{\mathbb{R}} \int_0^T \frac{\partial \rho}{\partial t} V(x, t) dt dx$$

Change the order of integration in I_2 and write it as

$$I_2 = \int_0^T \int_{\mathbb{R}} \rho \mu \frac{\partial V}{\partial x} dx dt$$

Use integration by parts on the integrand, with $u = \rho\mu$, $v' = \frac{\partial V}{\partial x}$ so that $u' = \frac{\partial(\rho\mu)}{\partial x}$, $v = V$

$$\int_{\mathbb{R}} \rho \mu \frac{\partial V}{\partial x} dx = \rho \mu V \big|_{\mathbb{R}} - \int_{\mathbb{R}} \frac{\partial(\rho\mu)}{\partial x} V dx$$

Hence the integral can be evaluated as

$$I_2 = - \int_0^T \int_{\mathbb{R}} \frac{\partial(\rho\mu)}{\partial x} V(x, t) dx dt$$

$$= - \int_{\mathbb{R}} \int_0^T \frac{\partial(\rho\mu)}{\partial x} V(x, t) dt dx$$

Finally, the evaluation of the integrand of I_3 requires the application of integration by parts on x twice. This is because in the integrand we want to get rid of the $\frac{\partial^2 V}{\partial x^2}$ term and end up with $V(x, t)$ only. Again, change the order of integration and write I_3 as

$$\frac{1}{2} \int_0^T \int_{\mathbb{R}} \rho \sigma^2 \frac{\partial^2 V}{\partial x^2} dx dt$$

For the first integration by parts use $u = \rho\sigma^2$, $v' = \frac{\partial^2 V}{\partial x^2}$ so that $u' = \frac{\partial(\rho\sigma^2)}{\partial x}$ and $v = \frac{\partial V}{\partial x}$. Hence the integrand can be written

$$\int_{\mathbb{R}} \rho\sigma^2 \frac{\partial^2 V}{\partial x^2} dx = \rho\sigma^2 \frac{\partial V}{\partial x}\Big|_{\mathbb{R}} - \int_{\mathbb{R}} \frac{\partial\left(\rho\sigma^2\right)}{\partial x} \frac{\partial V}{\partial x} dx$$

$$= -\int_{\mathbb{R}} \frac{\partial\left(\rho\sigma^2\right)}{\partial x} \frac{\partial V}{\partial x} dx$$

Apply integration by parts again, with $u = \frac{\partial(\rho\sigma^2)}{\partial x}$, $v' = \frac{\partial V}{\partial x}$, $u' = \frac{\partial^2(\rho\sigma^2)}{\partial x^2}$, $v = V$

$$-\int_{\mathbb{R}} \frac{\partial\left(\rho\sigma^2\right)}{\partial x} \frac{\partial V}{\partial x} dx = -\frac{\partial\left(\rho\sigma^2\right)}{\partial x} V\Big|_{\mathbb{R}} + \int_{\mathbb{R}} \frac{\partial^2\left(\rho\sigma^2\right)}{\partial x^2} V dx$$

$$= \int_{\mathbb{R}} \frac{\partial^2\left(\rho\sigma^2\right)}{\partial x^2} V(x,t) dx$$

This implies that I_3 can be written as

$$\frac{1}{2}\int_0^T \int_{\mathbb{R}} \frac{\partial^2\left(\rho\sigma^2\right)}{\partial x^2} V dx dt = \frac{1}{2}\int_{\mathbb{R}} \int_0^T \frac{\partial^2\left(\rho\sigma^2\right)}{\partial x^2} V(x,t) dt dx$$

We can substitute I_1, I_2 and I_3 in (6)

$$E\left[V\left(X_T, T\right)\right] - V\left(X_0, 0\right) = \int_{\mathbb{R}} \int_0^T V(x,t) \left[-\frac{\partial\rho}{\partial t} - \frac{\partial(\rho\mu)}{\partial x} + \frac{1}{2}\frac{\partial^2\left(\rho\sigma^2\right)}{\partial x^2}\right] dt dx$$

Since $V\left(X_t, t\right) = 0$ for $t \notin (0, T)$ we have $V\left(X_T, T\right) = V\left(X_0, 0\right) = 0$ so that $E\left[V\left(X_T, T\right)\right] - V\left(X_0\right) = 0$. This implies that the portion of the integrand in the brackets is zero

$$-\frac{\partial\rho}{\partial t} - \frac{\partial(\rho\mu)}{\partial x} + \frac{1}{2}\frac{\partial^2\left(\rho\sigma^2\right)}{\partial x^2} = 0$$

from which the Fokker-Planck equation can be obtained

$$\frac{\partial\rho}{\partial t} = -\frac{\partial(\rho\mu)}{\partial x} + \frac{1}{2}\frac{\partial^2\left(\rho\sigma^2\right)}{\partial x^2}$$

10.6   Breeden-Litzenberger - Solution

Question :   Derive the Breeden-Litzenberger Formula.

Solution :   The Breeden-Litzenberger formula connects the underlying distribution to the derivatives of call options with respect to the strike. We start with the call price expectation formula

$$C(S, K, T) = e^{-rT}\mathbb{E}\left(\left(S_T - K\right)^+\right) = e^{-rT}\int_K^\infty (x - k)p(x)dx$$

where $p(x)$ is the density function of S_T. We take the derivative with respect to K using the Leibniz formula (see page 91)

$$\frac{\partial C}{\partial K} = e^{-rT} \int_K^\infty -p(x)dx$$

We take the second derivative to get the Breeden-Litzenberger formula.

$$\frac{\partial^2 C}{\partial K^2} = e^{-rT} p(k)$$

10.7 Local Volatility - Solution

Question : Derive the Dupire Formula or Local Volatility.

Solution : It might be surprising but this question is sometimes asked in interview. Local volatility is such an industry standard that you absolutely need to know it after a few years as a quant. Remember that the local volatility $\sigma_{loc}(t, S_t)$ when injected in the process S_t

$$\frac{dS_t}{S_t} = (r(t) - q(t))dt + \sigma_{loc}(t, S_t)dW_t$$

matches the vanilla prices, or in other terms, the implied volatility surface, because option prices are actually the implied volatility surface. Dupire proved the existence and uniqueness of the local volatility surface in his seminal 1994 paper. The idea is to connect the stock dynamics to the stock distribution using the Fokker Planck equation, and then to the call prices using the Breeden Litzenberger formula.

So we start by assuming that the stock prices follow

$$\frac{dS_t}{S_t} = (r(t) - q(t))dt + \sigma(t, S_t)dW_t$$

So the Breeden-Litzenberger formula between times s and T, for a stock of spot value s, at time t, and discounting factor $D(t, T)$ (typically $D(t, T) = e^{r(T-t)}$) is

$$p(s, K, t, T) = \frac{1}{D(t, T)} \frac{\partial^2}{\partial K^2} C_t(s, K, T)$$

We apply Fokker-Planck to the stock

$$\frac{1}{2}\frac{\partial^2}{\partial x^2}\left[\sigma(t, x)^2 x^2 p(x_0, x, t_0, t)\right] - (r(t) - q(t))\frac{\partial}{\partial x}\left[xp(x_0, x, t_0, t)\right]$$

$$-\frac{\partial}{\partial t}p(x_0, x, t_0, t) = 0$$

We multiply this by $D(t_0, t)(x - K)^+$ and integrate from $x = K$ to $x = \infty$ to get

$$\frac{1}{2}D(t_0, t)\int_K^\infty \frac{\partial^2}{\partial x^2}\left[\sigma(t, x)^2 x^2 p(x_0, x, t_0, t)\right](x - K)dx$$

$$-(r(t) - q(t))D(t_0, t)\int_K^\infty \frac{\partial}{\partial x}\left[xp(x_0, x, t_0, t)\right](x - K)dx \qquad (7)$$

$$-D(t_0, t)\int_K^\infty \frac{\partial}{\partial t}p(x_0, x, t_0, t)(x - K) = 0$$

The first term in equation (7) can be integrated by parts and using the Breeden-Litzenberger formula it can be rewritten as

$$\tfrac{1}{2}\sigma(t,K)^2 K^2 \frac{\partial^2}{\partial K^2} C_{t_0}(x_0, K, t) \tag{8}$$

The second term in equation (7) can be integrated by parts and using the integral version of the Breeden-Litzenberger formula it becomes

$$(r(t) - q(t)) \left(C_{t_0}(x_0, K, t) - K \frac{\partial}{\partial K} C_{t_0}(x_0, K, t) \right) \tag{9}$$

The last term in equation (7) can be integrated directly and using

$$D_t(t_0, t) = -r(t)D(t_0, t)$$

we obtain

$$-\left(r(t)C(x, K, t) + \frac{\partial}{\partial t} C_{t_0}(x_0, K, t) \right) \tag{10}$$

After subtituting the three terms and rearranging equation (7) we obtain the Dupire Formula

$$\sigma(t,K)^2 = \frac{(r(t) - q(t))K\frac{\partial}{\partial K}C_{t_0}(x_0, K, t) + \frac{\partial}{\partial t}C_{t_0}(x_0, K, t) + q(t)C_{t_0}(x_0, K, t)}{\tfrac{1}{2}K^2\frac{\partial^2}{\partial K^2}C_{t_0}(x_0, K, t)}$$

Usually we find it written in this compact form

$$\sigma_{\mathrm{loc}}(t,K)^2 = \frac{\frac{\partial C}{\partial t} + (r(t) - q(t))K\frac{\partial C}{\partial K} + q(t)C}{\tfrac{1}{2}K^2\frac{\partial^2 C}{\partial K^2}} = \frac{C_t + (r - q)KC_k + qC}{\tfrac{1}{2}K^2 C_{KK}}$$

10.8   Black Scholes Equation - Solution

Question :   Derive the Black Scholes equation.

Solution :   We consider a financial option on a stock S_t of value $V(S_t, t)$. We construct a self-financed portfolio with the option and a Δ hedging amount of stock.

$$P = V(S, t) + \Delta S$$

The stock has the usual dynamics

$$\frac{\mathrm{d}S_t}{S_t} = r\mathrm{d}t + \sigma \mathrm{d}W_t$$

The self-financing portfolio condition is

$$dP = dV + \Delta dS \tag{11}$$

And the non arbitrage condition gives us

$$dP = rPdt \tag{12}$$

We apply Itô on V, and combining (11) and (12) we have

$$V_t dt + V_S dS + \frac{1}{2} V_{SS} d\langle S \rangle_t + \Delta dS = rP dt$$

Therefore we have the hedging amount Δ

$$\Delta = -V_S$$

and

$$V_t dt + \frac{1}{2} V_{SS} d\langle S \rangle_t = rV dt - rSV_S dt$$

We use the stock dynamics and simplify the dt

$$V_t + \frac{1}{2} V_{SS} \sigma^2 S^2 = rV - rSV_S$$

We obtain the Black Scholes equation, usually written

$$V_t + \frac{1}{2} V_{SS} \sigma^2 S^2 + rSV_S - rV = 0$$

It is sometimes found in its forward version

$$V_t + \frac{1}{2} V_{FF} \sigma^2 F^2 - rV = 0$$

which is derived using the derivation rule

$$\frac{\partial V(F, t)}{\partial t} = \frac{\partial V}{\partial t} + \frac{\partial F}{\partial t} \frac{\partial V}{\partial F} = V_t + rFV_F$$

Chapter 11

Math Cheatsheet

Math Cheatsheet

11.1 Normal Distribution

$$X \sim \mathcal{N}\left(\mu, \sigma^2\right)$$

$$f_X(x) = \frac{1}{\sqrt{2\pi}\sigma} \exp\left(-\frac{(x-\mu)^2}{2\sigma^2}\right)$$

11.2 Correlation

The population correlation coefficient $\rho_{X,Y}$ between two random variables X and Y with standard deviations σ_X and σ_Y is defined as

$$\rho_{X,Y} = \frac{\text{cov}(X, Y)}{\sigma_X \sigma_Y}$$

11.3 Brownian Motion

A Brownian motion is a stochastic process $\{B_t\}_{t \geq 0+}$ with the following properties:

- $B_0 = 0$

- The function $t \to B_t$ is almost surely continuous in t

- The process $\{B_t\}_{t \geq 0}$ has stationary, independent increments

- The increment $B_{t+s} - B_s$ has the $\mathcal{N}(0, t)$ distribution

11.4 σ-algebra

Let Ω be a set. A collection $\mathcal{A}$ of subsets of Ω is a σ-algebra on Ω, if and only if it satisfies all the following properties:

- $\Omega, \emptyset \in \mathcal{A}$

- For all $A \in \mathcal{A}$, $A^c \in \mathcal{A}$

- For all sequence $(A_n)_{n=1}^{\infty}$ of elements of $\mathcal{A}$, $\cup_{n=1}^{\infty} A_n \in \mathcal{A}$

11.5 Martingale

An $(\mathcal{F}_t)$-adapted, real-valued process M is called a martingale (with respect to the filtration $(\mathcal{F}_t)$) if

- $\mathrm{E}\,|M_t| < \infty$ for all $t \in T$

- $\mathrm{E}\,(M_t|\mathcal{F}_s) \stackrel{\text{a.s.}}{=} M_s$ for all $s \leq t$

11.6 Girsanov

Let $B_t, 0 \leq t \leq T$ be a Brownian motion on a probability space $(\Omega, \mathcal{F}, P)$, and let $\mathcal{F}_t, 0 \leq t \leq T$, be a filtration for this Brownian motion. Let a_t be an adapted process. Define

$$Z_t = \exp\left(-\int_0^t a_u dB_u - \frac{1}{2}\int_0^t a_u^2 du\right)$$

$$\tilde{B}_t = B_t + \int_0^t a_u du$$

and the probability $\tilde{P}$ equivalent to P defined by

$$\tilde{P}(A) = \int_A Z(\omega) dP(\omega)$$

and assume that

$$E\left[\int_0^t a_u^2 Z_u^2 du\right] < +\infty$$

Then under the probability $\tilde{P}$ the process $\tilde{B}$ is a Brownian motion.

11.7 Itô Process

A process X_t is said to be an Itô process if there exist progressively measurable processes α_t and β_t such that

$$\int_0^t \left(|\alpha_s| + \beta_s^2\right) ds < \infty, \text{ a.s.}$$

$$X_t = X_0 + \int_0^t \alpha_s ds + \int_0^t \beta_s dB_s$$

11.8 Itô's Lemma

Let $f(t, x)$ be a real-valued function whose second-order partial derivatives are continuous. Let $(X_t)_{t \geq 0}$ be an Itô process, Then

$$df(t, X) = \frac{\partial f}{\partial t}dt + \frac{\partial f}{\partial x}dX + \frac{1}{2}\frac{\partial^2 f}{\partial x^2}d\langle X\rangle_t$$

In practice, it is more convenient to use the notation

$$df = f_t dt + f_X dX + \frac{1}{2}f_{XX}d\langle X\rangle_t$$

11.9 Levy Theorem

Let M_t be a martingale with continuous sample paths and $M_0 = 0$. Then

$$d\langle M\rangle_t = dt \iff M \text{ is a Brownian motion}$$

11.10   Martingale representation Theorem

Let B_t be a Brownian motion and $\mathcal{F}_t$ the augmented filtration generated by B_t. If X is an $\mathcal{F}_\infty$-measurable square integrable random variable, then there is a unique $\mathcal{F}_t$-adapted predictable process ϕ, such that

$$X = \mathbb{E}[X] + \int_0^\infty \phi_s dB_s$$

11.11   Doob's Optional Sampling Theorem

If M is a martingale and S, T are stopping times with

$$S \leq T \text{ a.s. and } \mathbb{E}\,|M_T| < +\infty$$

then

$$\mathbb{E}\,[M_T|\mathcal{F}_S] = M_S$$

11.12   Doob's Optional-Stopping Theorem

Let $(\Omega, \Sigma, \mathbf{P})$ be a probability space, $\mathcal{F} = \{F_n\}$ a filtration on Ω, and $X = \{X_n\}$ a martingale with respect to $\mathcal{F}$. Let τ be a stopping time. Suppose that any one of the following conditions holds:

- There is a positive integer N such that $\tau(\omega) \leq N$ for all $\omega \in \Omega$

- There is a positive real number K such that

$$|X_n(\omega)| < K$$

  for all n and all $\omega \in \Omega$, and τ is almost surely finite.

- $\mathbb{E}(\tau) < \infty$, and there is a positive real number K such that

$$|X_n(\omega) - X_{n-1}(\omega)| < K$$

  for all n and all $\omega \in \Omega$ Then X_T is integrable, and

$$\mathbb{E}\,(X_\tau) = \mathbb{E}\,(X_0)$$

11.13   Long-term behavior of trajectories

Let $\{B_t\}_{t \in [0,\infty)}$ be a Brownian motion. Then,

$$\limsup_{t \to \infty} \frac{B_t}{\sqrt{t}} = \infty, \ a.s$$

and

$$\liminf_{t \to \infty} \frac{B_t}{\sqrt{t}} = -\infty, \ a.s$$

11.14   Stopping Time

A (generalized) random variable T is called a stopping time if $T : \Omega \longrightarrow \mathbb{Z}_+ \cup \{\infty\}$ satisfies $\{T \leq n\} \in \mathcal{F}_n$.

11.15   Hitting Times (First Passage Times)

Let $T_a = \min\{t : B(t) = a\}$ be the first time the standard Brownian motion process hits a. Using the reflection principle we can prove that

$$P\left(T_a \leq t\right) = 2P(B(t) \geq a) = 2 - 2\Phi(a/\sqrt{t})$$

$$\lim_{t \to \infty} P\left(T_a \leq t\right) = 1$$

11.16   Itô's Isometry

Let B_t be a Brownian Motion and X_t a stochastic process

$$\mathrm{E}\left[\left(\int_0^T X_t dB_t\right)^2\right] = \mathrm{E}\left[\int_0^T X_t^2 dt\right]$$

11.17   Bayes' theorem

$$P(A|B) = \frac{P(B|A)P(A)}{P(B)}$$

where A and B are events and $P(B) \neq 0$

11.18   Self-financing Portfolios

A portfolio, or trading strategy, is any predictable process

$$\phi = (\phi_0, \ldots, \phi_n)$$

Its corresponding value process is

$$V(t) = V(t; \phi) := \sum_{i=0}^n \phi_i(t) S_i(t)$$

The portfolio ϕ is called self-financing (for S) if the stochastic integrals

$$\int_0^t \phi_i(u) dS_i(u), \quad i = 0, \ldots, n$$

are well defined and

$$dV(t; \phi) = \sum_{i=0}^n \phi_i(t) dS_i(t)$$

11.19 Uniform Integrability Test Functions

A function $\psi : [0, \infty) \to [0, \infty)$ is called a u.i. (uniform integrability) test function if ψ is increasing, convex (i.e. $\psi(\lambda x + (1 - \lambda)y) \leq \lambda\psi(x) + (1 - \lambda)\psi(y)$ for all $x, y \in [0, \infty), \lambda \in [0, 1]$) and

$$\lim_{x \to \infty} \frac{\psi(x)}{x} = \infty$$

So for example $\psi(x) = x^p$ is a u.i. test function if $p > 1$.

11.20 Uniform Integrability Theorem

The family $\{f_j\}_{j \in J}$ is uniformly integrable if and only if there is a u.i. test function ψ such that

$$\sup_{j \in J} \left\{ \int \psi\left(|f_j|\right) dP \right\} < \infty$$

11.21 Doob's martingale convergence theorem

Let N_t be a right-continuous supermartingale. Then the following are equivalent:

1. $\{N_t\}_{t \geq 0}$ is uniformly integrable

2. There exists $N \in L^1(P)$ such that $N_t \to N$ a.e. (P) and $N_t \to N$ in $L^1(P)$, i.e. $\int |N_t - N| \, dP \to 0$ as $t \to \infty$

11.22 Local Volatility

The local volatility is defined as

$$\sigma_{\text{loc}}(t, K)^2 = \frac{C_t + (r - q)KC_k + qC}{\frac{1}{2}K^2 C_{KK}}$$

If we express the option price as a function of the forward price

$$F_t = S_0 e^{\int_0^T \mu_t dt}$$

where μ_t represents the risk-neutral drift of the stock process, we get the forward version of local volatility

$$\sigma_{\text{loc}}(t, K)^2 = \frac{C_t}{\frac{1}{2}K^2 C_{KK}}$$

11.23 Breeden-Litzenberger

First order form

$$\frac{\partial C}{\partial K} = e^{-rT} \int_K^\infty -p(x)dx$$

Second order form

$$\frac{\partial^2 C}{\partial K^2} = e^{-rT} p(k)$$

11.24   Fokker-Planck

$$\frac{\partial \rho}{\partial t} = -\frac{\partial(\rho\mu)}{\partial x} + \frac{1}{2}\frac{\partial^2 \left(\rho\sigma^2\right)}{\partial x^2}$$

11.25   Vanilla Options

Call option

$$C = S_0 e^{-qT}\phi(d_1) - Ke^{-rT}\phi(d_2)$$

$$d_1 = \frac{\ln\left(\frac{S_0}{K}\right) + (r-q)T + \frac{\sigma^2 T}{2}}{\sigma\sqrt{T}} \quad , \quad d_2 = \frac{\ln\left(\frac{S_0}{K}\right) + (r-q)T - \frac{\sigma^2 T}{2}}{\sigma\sqrt{T}}$$

Put option

$$P = Ke^{-rT}\phi(-d_2) - S_0 e^{-qT}\phi(-d_1)$$

11.26   Reflection Principle

Let W_t a Brownian motion, and $a > 0$, then the reflection principle states:

$$\mathbb{P}\left(\sup_{0 \le s \le t} W(s) \ge a\right) = 2\mathbb{P}(W(t) \ge a)$$

11.27   Tanaka's Fromula

$$|B_t| = \int_0^t \mathrm{sgn}(B_s)\, dB_s + L_t$$

where B_t is the standard Brownian motion, sgn denotes the sign function and L_t is its local time at 0 (the local time spent by B at 0 before time t) given by the L_2-limit

$$L_t = \lim_{\varepsilon \downarrow 0} \frac{1}{2\varepsilon}|\{s \in [0,t]| B_s \in (-\varepsilon, +\varepsilon)\}|$$

11.28   Symmetric Matrices

Any symmetric matrix A $(A = A^T)$

- has only real eigenvalues

- is always diagonalizable

- has orthogonal eigenvectors

11.29   Semidefinite Positive Matrices

The symmetric matrix A is said positive semidefinite $(A \ge 0)$ if all its eigenvalues are non negative.

11.30 Useful Taylor Series

$$\frac{1}{1-x} = 1 + x + x^2 + x^3 + x^4 + \ldots$$

$$\left(\frac{1}{1-x}\right)' = \frac{1}{(1-x)^2} = 1 + 2x + 3x^2 + 4x^3 + 5x^4 + \ldots$$

$$e^x = 1 + x + \frac{x^2}{2!} + \frac{x^3}{3!} + \frac{x^4}{4!} + \ldots$$

$$\cos x = 1 - \frac{x^2}{2!} + \frac{x^4}{4!} - \frac{x^6}{6!} + \frac{x^8}{8!} - \ldots$$

$$\sin x = x - \frac{x^3}{3!} + \frac{x^5}{5!} - \frac{x^7}{7!} + \frac{x^9}{9!} - \ldots$$

11.31 Leibniz Integral Rule

Theorem. Let $f(x,t)$ be a function such that both $f(x,t)$ and its partial derivative $f_x(x,t)$ are continuous in t and x in some region of the (x,t)-plane, including $a(x) \le t \le b(x)$, $x_0 \le x \le 1$. Also suppose that the functions $a(x)$ and $b(x)$ are both continuous and both have continuous derivatives for $x_0 \le x \le x_1$. Then, for $x_0 \le x \le x_1$,

$$\frac{d}{dx}\left(\int_{a(x)}^{b(x)} f(x,t)dt\right) = f(x,b(x))\,b'(x) - f(x,a(x)) + \int_{a(x)}^{b(x)} \frac{\partial}{\partial x} f(x,t)dt$$

A Humble Request

Dear valued reader,

We are, Editions Ducourt, a small publishing company and without your support we would not exist.

Therefore we make a humble request - if you enjoy this book, please spare a few minutes to leave us a review on this book's Amazon product page.

Each and every one of your reviews is paramount to the success of the book as its visibility is impacted by the Amazon algorithm.

We are forever grateful for your support and we hope we have succeeded in providing you with a very special book.

Sincerely
Editions Ducourt 51

Index

σ-algebra, 85
Breeden-Litzenberger, 67, 89
Fokker-Planck, 90
Fokker-Planck , 67
Itô Process, 86
Itô's Isometry, 88
Itô's Lemma, 86

Bayes, 88
Black Scholes Equation, 68
Brownian Bridge, 24
Brownian Motion, 85

Call Option, 67
Chooser Option, 41
Class, 55
Compound Option, 42
Correlation, 85

Doob, 89
Doob's Optional-Stopping Theorem, 87

Exchange Option, 41

Forward Start Option, 41
Friend class, 55

Girsanov, 86
Greeks, 67

Hash, 56
Hybrid, 67

Leibniz Integral Rule, 91
Levy Theorem, 86

Local Volatility, 67, 89
Lognormal, 23

Martingale, 24, 85
Martingale representation Theorem, 87

Normal Distribution, 85

Ornstein Uhlenbeck, 67

Prime, 3

Ramsey, 3
Reflection Principle, 90

Self, 56
Self-financing Portfolio, 88
Semidefinite Matrix, 90
Singleton, 55
Sorting algorithm, 55
Struct, 55
Symmetric Matrices, 90

Taylor Series, 91

Vasicek, 67